A Greek Hupogrammon

Other items available to accompany A Greek Hupogrammon Copybook:

A Greek Alphabetarion – A Primer for Teaching How to Read, Write, & Pronounce Ancient & Biblical Greek. This book teaches the Greek alphabet in alphabetical order, letter by letter, using a rhythmic cadence to aid the student's memorization. Then it teaches the alphabet in phonetic order, classifying each letter by its sound. It is formatted to make it easier for parents to teach their children, and for older students to learn by themselves. It includes a syllabary (practice blending consonants and vowels) and a chrestomathy (practice reading sample passages). It is suitable for all ages, child through adult, in homeschools, private schools, colleges, and seminaries. A pronunciation CD is included.

Greek Alphabet Flash Cards for practice and drill. These cards show both the capital and the lowercase Greek letters on one side and the correct pronunciation on the reverse side.

Greek Alphabet Banner for mounting on a wall. The banner displays both the capital and lowercase Greek letters.

Homeschool Greek – A Thorough Self-Teaching Grammar of Biblical Greek. This grammar teaches each grammatical concept in English before teaching the similar or dissimilar concept in Greek. Biblical expressions from the New Testament and Proverbs are used for examples and are committed to memory. Vocabulary Cards, Greek Reader, Diagnostic Tests, and Audio Tapes are included. This grammar is the next step after mastering *A Greek Alphabetarion.*

Also by Harvey Bluedorn:

A Basic Exegetical and Expository Grammar of Biblical Greek, 1987

Vocabulary Bridges from English to Latin and Greek, 1994

Teaching the Trivium: Christian Homeschooling in a Classical Style, 2001

Ancient History from Primary Sources: A Literary Timeline, 2003

Handy English Encoder Decoder: All the Spelling and Phonics Rules You Could Ever Want to Know, 1994, 2004

A Greek Alphabetarion: A Primer for Teaching How to Read, Write, & Pronounce Ancient & Biblical Greek, 1993, 2004

Homeschool Greek [aka Self-Study Greek]: A Thorough Self-Teaching Grammar of Biblical Greek, 1996, 2004

Stephanus 2000 in Unicode: The Traditional Greek Text with Full Diacritical Markings, 2003

A Greek Hupogrammon

A Beginner's Copybook for the Greek Alphabet with Pronunciations

by Harvey Bluedorn

Designed to Accompany

A Greek Alphabetarion

October 2005
Trivium Pursuit

A GREEK HUPOGRAMMON
by Harvey Bluedorn

Library of Congress Control Number: 2005901148
ISBN 1-933228-01-6

Trivium Pursuit
PMB 168, 429 Lake Park Boulevard
Muscatine, Iowa, 52761
309-537-3641
www.triviumpursuit.com

Cover by Richard LaPierre.

> *"You shall not muzzle an ox while it is threshing grain."*
> *"The worker deserves his just compensation."* (1 Timothy 5:18)
> *"You shall not steal."*
> *"You shall love your neighbor as yourself."* (Romans 13:9)

Table of Contents

The Greek Alphabet

Greek Vowel Combinations

Chrestomathy

Answer Key to Exercises

Introduction

Ancient students learned to read and to write the Greek language by carefully examining and copying a *copyhead* or *hupogrammon* (pronounced "hoo-poe-GRAH-moan" in Greek, though in English we might place the accent on the second syllable: "hoo-POE-grah-moan"). First Peter 2:21 uses such a copyhead as a figure of speech: "Christ also suffered on our behalf, leaving behind *an example for us to copy* (literally: *a copyhead*), in order that you should trace over His tracks." ***A Greek Hupogrammon Copybook*** is a consumable workbook designed to help the beginning student to trace through the fundamental steps of reading and writing the ancient Greek language.

This workbook is laid out in two-page spreads. Most lessons have only one two-page spread. Young students may do up to one spread per day. Older or more ambitious students may do two or more spreads per day.

We have sought to cover the Greek alphabet and pronunciation system in a simple yet comprehensive way. Older and more experienced students (ten years old and upward) should be able to progress through the copybook without further explanation or help. Students younger than this may require extra help. Also, if more practice is desired, the student may use additional paper or a writing board.

Though the lessons in this copybook can be used without any accompanying text, they are designed to correspond with the more extensive textbook, *A Greek Alphabetarion*. A younger student could first learn the basics by going through the *Hupogrammon*, then review the same material more carefully and extensively by going through the *Alphabetarion*. An older student might use both books together. In this case, we suggest that the student first read the appropriate section of the *Alphabetarion* (and listen to the corresponding audio track on the compact disk), then do the exercises in the *Hupogrammon Copybook*.

We have designed exercises 1) to give the student practice in writing Greek letters, 2) to familiarize the student with the look of Greek and to help him to identify and distinguish letters, and 3) to cause the student to associate certain sounds or pronunciations with each letter symbol. Some of the exercises may seem difficult to an eight-year-old, and some exercises may seem easy to a twelve-year-old, but the idea of all of the exercises is to provide the student with an abundance of practice.

At the end of this copybook is an answer key to the exercises, organized by page spreads and identified by exercise numbers.

The Greek Alphabet

This letter is called Alpha (as in "fäll fär").

1 Practice writing capital and lowercase Alpha on the page to the right. Say the name out loud each time you write the letter.

2 Underline the Alphas in the following Greek lines and sentences.

John 8:39-40 απεκριθησαν και ειπον αυτω, ο πατηρ ημων Αβρααμ εστι. λεγει αυτοις ο Ιησους, ει τεκνα του Αβρααμ ητε, τα εργα του Αβρααμ εποιειτε αν. νυν δε ζητειτε με αποκτειναι, ανθρωπον ος την αληθειαν υμιν λελαληκα, ην ηκουσα παρα του Θεου· ...

The sound of Alpha is like the sound of the English letter A in yacht and yawn.

A							
α							
A							
α							
A							
α							
A							
α							

3 In the following sentences, underline the English letters which sound like Alpha.
Example: lawn lot

Father called to talk to mama.
They bought tickets for the drama.
Halt in the name of the law.
Her daughter taught her to totter.
Otto ought to audit his autographs.

Greek vowel sounds may be *short* or *long*. The sound of *short* Alpha is like the sound of the English letter A in y<u>a</u>cht. The sound of *long* Alpha is like the sound of the English letters AW in y<u>aw</u>n. The sound in y<u>aw</u>n lasts a little longer than the sound in y<u>a</u>cht.

In English, we do not usually pay close attention to how long we hold a vowel sound, so we aren't always consistent in the way we pronounce words. In Greek, there are rules for whether a vowel sound should be pronounced *short* or *long*, but we can't explain these rules here.

4 In the following list of English words, underline the vowels which you think sound like Alpha – whether long or short. Then go back and draw an additional *macron* ¯ over those letters which you might sometimes lengthen like the *long* sound of Alpha. (This can sometimes be hard to tell – we pronounce words a little differently in different sentences.) Example: g<u>o</u>t ll<u>ā</u>m<u>a</u>

Anna aria drama mama
Omaha papa banana
catawba aardvark lollipop polygon
law withdrawal dawdle
squawk scrawl awkward
ah hurrah pariah sahib father
alcohol almond walnut false tall talk all
alter ball balk balm fall asphalt
taught daughter sauce sausage fraud
pause vault pauper popper authentic
tot cloth respond coffee bronze along
volcano involve doll gone hollow solid
sorry borrow tomorrow knowledge bomb
Otto ought bought audit odd auto trough
Harvard carpet carnival departure

You should now see that English does have the long and short sound, but it is often hard to tell. You may assume that all Alphas in this book are to be pronounced short unless we show you otherwise with a macron (ᾱ) over the letter.

β Β

This letter is called Beta (as in "bāy täll").

1 Practice writing capital and lowercase Beta on the page to the right. Say the name out loud each time you write the letter.

2 Underline the Betas in the following Greek lines and sentences.

John 18:39-40 εστι δε συνηθεια υμιν, ινα ενα υμιν απολυσω εν τω πασχα· βουλεσθε ουν υμιν απολυσω τον βασιλεα των Ιουδαιων; εκραυγασαν ουν παλιν παντες, λεγοντες, μη τουτον, αλλα τον Βαραββαν· ην δε ο Βαραββας ληστης.

The sound of Beta is like the sound of the English letter B in bob.

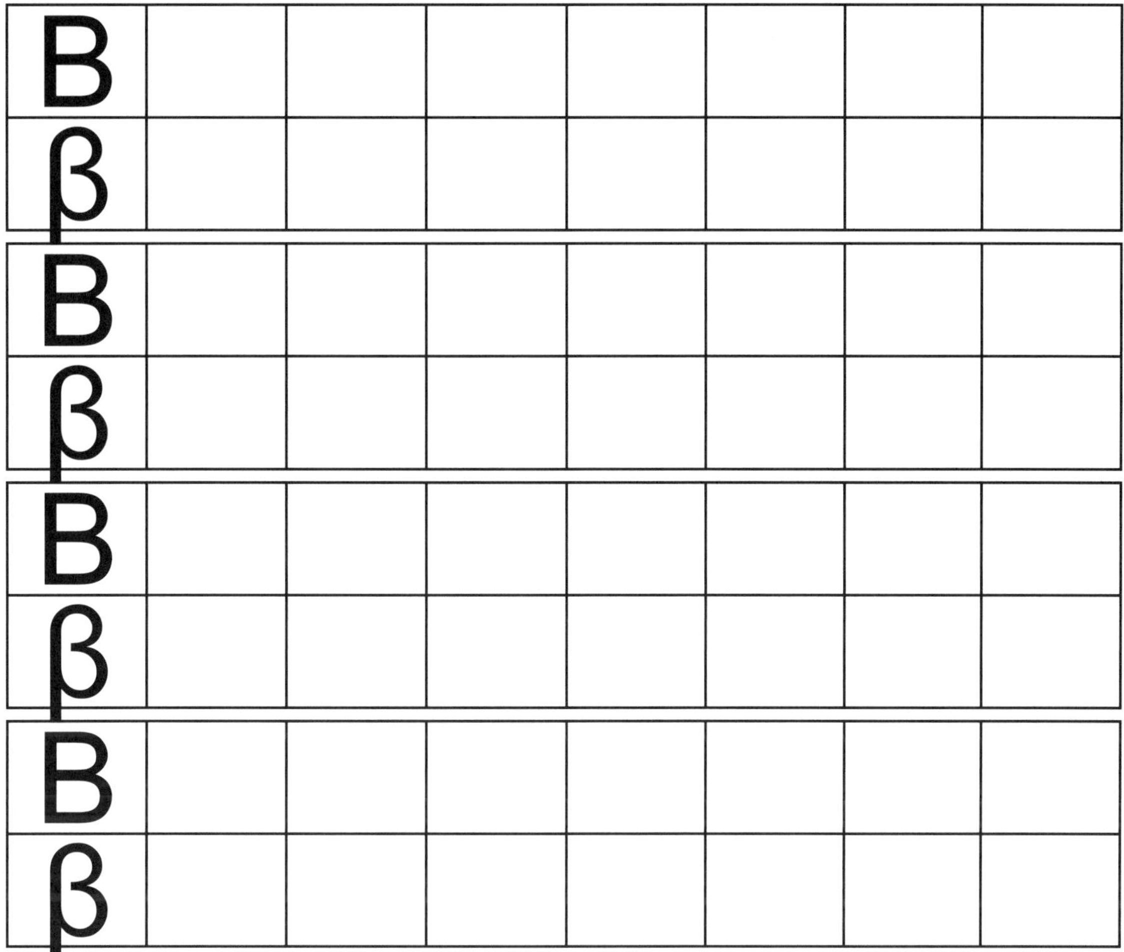

3 In the following sentences, underline the English letters which sound like Beta.

Example: boat lobby

Caleb wrote the subtle subtitle.
Abbey obviously doubts the story.
Ma Hubbard's cupboard was bare.
Bobby buys baby buggy bumpers.
Below, Blain blows blue balloons.

γ Γ

This letter is called Gamma (rhyming with "drämä" almost as in "gäll mŏb").

1 Practice writing capital and lowercase Gamma on the page to the right. Say the name out loud each time you write the letter.

2 Underline the Gammas in the following Greek lines and sentences.

John 7:51-52 μη ο νομος ημων κρινει τον ανθρωπον, εαν μη ακουση παρ αυτου προτερον, και γνω τι ποιει; απεκριθησαν και ειπον αυτω, μη και συ εκ της Γαλιλαιας ει; ερευνησον και ιδε, οτι προφητης εκ της Γαλιλαιας ουκ εγηγερται.

The sound of Gamma is like the sound of the English letter G in gag (not like the G in ginger).

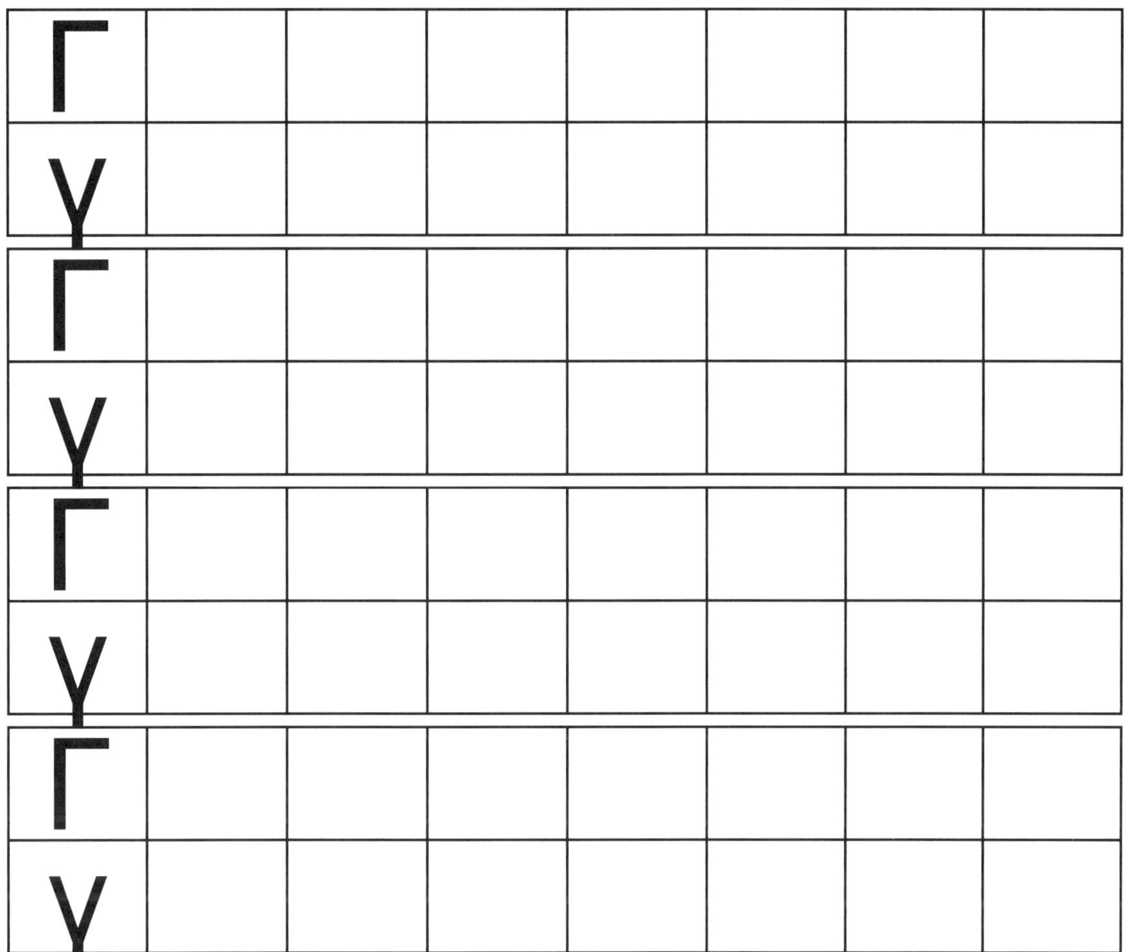

3 In the following sentences, underline the English letters which sound like Gamma.

Example: gargle boggle

Gorgeous George grew bigger.
Great green gobs of greasy grime.
A ghost was aghast at the laugh.
He sang as he sank in the sand.
Lang links lynx with lingering lions.

When followed by a palatal sound (like the sound of G in go, or the sound of K in kit), the sound of Gamma is like the sound of the English letters NG in sing, or the letter N in sink.

4 In the following list of English words, underline the English letters which represent the hard "G" sound of Gamma, then place a tilde ˜ over letters with the "NG" sound of Gamma. Example: gañg liñk

gaggle egg exaggerate leggings
binge bing bingo banger anger hungry
ghost weight ghetto cough aghast
through spaghetti enough sorghum
singer longer longitude single
ink zinc ingot links lynx anchor rancor
give ginger gear range geese
garage gorgeous baggage suggest
negligent diaphragm fragment sign
pregnant engage geography

sanction tanker tangent anxious
length conquer function distinct
guess guernsey vogue penguin guild

Later we will show you which Greek letters represent a palatal sound. (The *GREEK ALPHABETARION* explains which Greek letters represent a palatal sound.) When Gamma precedes these letters, then Gamma represents the sound of the English letters NG.

δ Δ

This letter is called Delta (as in "dĕalt ŏn").

1 Practice writing capital and lowercase Delta on the page to the right. Say the name out loud each time you write the letter.

2 Underline the Deltas in the following Greek lines and sentences.

John 6:70-71 απεκριθη αυτοις ο Ιησους, ουκ εγω υμας τους δωδεκα εξελεξαμην, και εξ υμων εις Διαβολος εστιν; ελεγε δε τον Ιουδαν Σιμωνος Ισκαριωτην· ουτος γαρ ημελλεν αυτον παραδιδοναι, εις ων εκ των δωδεκα.

The sound of Delta is like the sound of the English letter D in dad.

Δ							
δ							
Δ							
δ							
Δ							
δ							
Δ							
δ							

3 In the following sentences, underline the English letters which sound like Delta.

Example: ladder fads

Daddy docks his boat at the deck.
Handsome soldiers are doing duty.
The judge adjourned the jury trial.
The blind man had made fudge.
We dwell in a dry and arid land.

ε Ε

This letter is called Epsilon (as in "adĕpts ĭll ōwn").

1 Practice writing capital and lowercase Epsilon on the page to the right. Say the name out loud each time you write the letter.

2 Underline the Epsilons in the following Greek lines and sentences.

John 19:19-20 εγραψε δε και τιτλον ο Πιλατος, και εθηκεν επι του σταυρου· ην δε γεγραμμενον, Ιησους ο Ναζωραιος ο βασιλευς των Ιουδαιων. τουτον ουν τον τιτλον πολλοι ανεγνωσαν των Ιουδαιων ... και ην γεγραμμενον Εβραιστι, Ελληνιστι, Ρωμαιστι.

The sound of Epsilon is like the sound of the English letter E in whet.

E							
ε							
E							
ε							
E							
ε							
E							
ε							

3 In the following sentences, underline the English letters which sound like Epsilon.

Example: bed bread

He exits every evening event.

The cafe sold steak and eggs.

Ed decided he called too early.

We cannot guess the next answer.

A video leopard is in jeopardy.

Ϝ Ϝ

This letter is called Digamma (almost rhymes with "muddy gäll mŏp).

1 Practice writing capital and lowercase Digamma on the page to the right. Say the name out loud each time you write the letter.

The letter Digamma was obsolete even in ancient times, but it served a place in the numerical system.

2 Underline the Digammas in the following list of vocabulary words taken from ancient Greek. English definitions and English cognates are in parentheses.

ϝοῖνος (wine), ϝέργον (work, ergonomics), ϝιδεῖν (to see, video), ϝρήγνυμι (to break into pieces, fragment), ᾠϝόν (egg, ovum), ὀϝίς (a sheep, ovine), ϝεαρινός (belonging to spring, vernal), ἀκοϝή (sound, acoustic), ἀρόϝω (to plough, arable land)

The sounds of Digamma were probably like the letters F and W in off, of, whet, wet.

3 In the following sentences, underline the English letters which sound like Digamma. Example: foxglove when well.

When will we ever offer enough?
Who were those two suave men?
Wow, what a fine vocal choir.
Juan was one tough fellow.
Very few find what will work.

1 Write the English name for each Greek letter and write its lowercase form.

Α	Alpha	α
Β		
Γ		
Δ		
Ε		
F		

2 Underline the letters in the English words on the right which represent the sound (or sounds) of the Greek letter to its left.

α – all Audrey sad sod bought

β – bill doubt thumb obvious

γ – signal sign sing singe finger

δ – soldier daddy judge handsome

ε – hero head jet evening baked

3 Write the number of the Greek phonetic spelling on the left which matches the English word on the right.

0. δαγ ———————	_0_ dog
1. βαδ	__ Bob
2. αδ	__ ebb
3. δεδ	__ egg
4. βαγ	__ Deb
5. γαβ	__ daw
6. βαβ	__ odd
7. γαδ	__ Ed
8. εγ	__ dead
9. δα	__ bog
10. εβ	__ beg
11. εδ	__ gob
12. δαβ	__ baud
13. δεβ	__ bed
14. βεγ	__ daub
15. βεδ	__ God

ζ Z

This letter is called Dzeta (as in "frien<u>ds āte äl</u>l").

1 Practice writing capital and lowercase Dzeta on the page to the right. Say the name out loud each time you write the letter.

2 Underline the Dzetas in the following Greek lines and sentences.

Matthew 1:12 ...Σαλαθιηλ δε εγεννησε τον Ζοροβαβελ· Ζοροβαβελ δε εγεννησε τον Αβιουδ· ... Ελιακειμ δε εγεννησε τον Αζωρ· Αζωρ δε εγεννησε τον Σαδωκ· ... Ελιουδ δε εγεννησε τον Ελεαζαρ· Ελεαζαρ δε εγεννησε τον Ματθαν· ...

The sound of Dzeta is like the sound of the English letters DZ in a<u>dz</u>e.

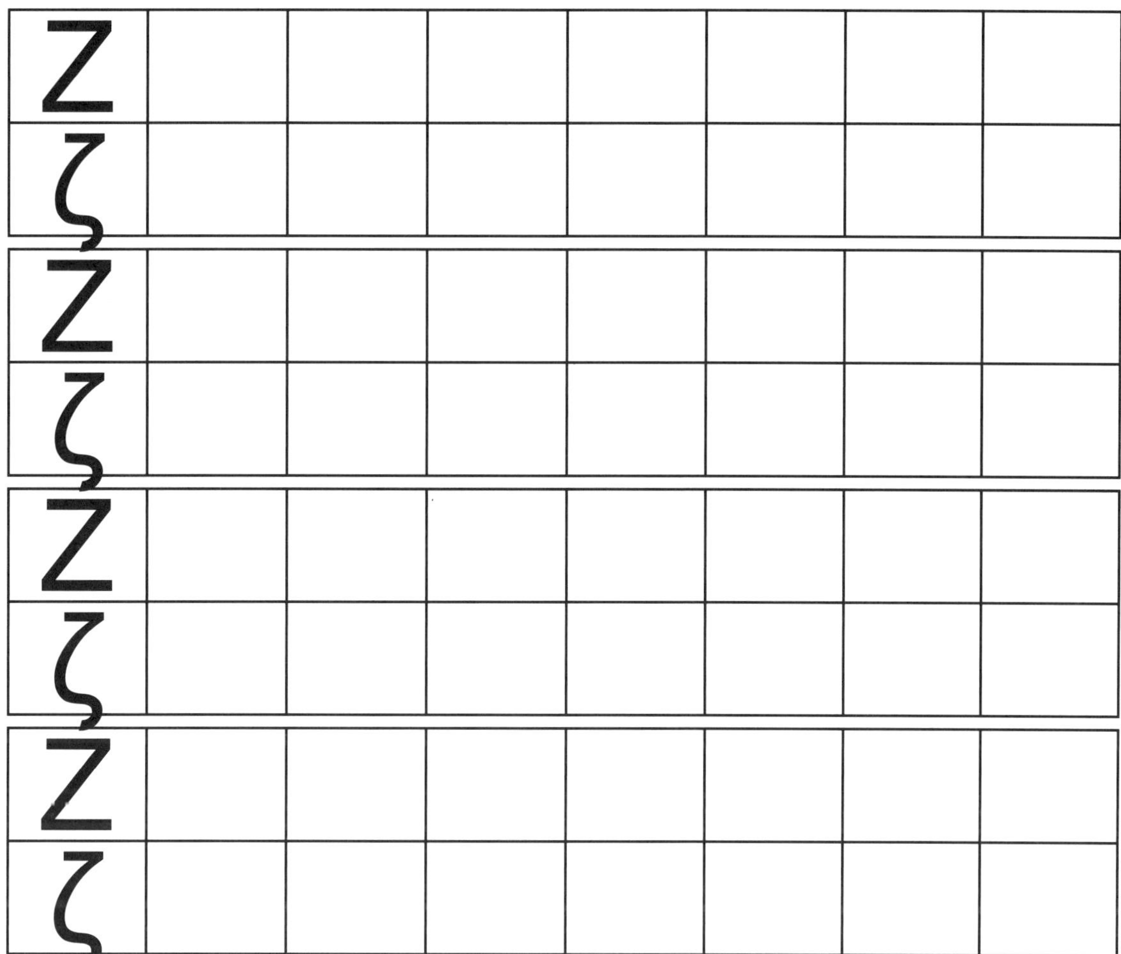

3 In thc following sentences, underline the English letters which sound like Dzeta.
Example: a<u>ds</u> frien<u>ds</u>

Unusual floods ruin the foods.
Buds on trees trigger his asthma.
He adds numbers, then divides.
His letter ends in poetic stanzas.
Zelda stands on her hands.

η Η

This letter is called Eta (as in "āte äll").

1 Practice writing capital and lowercase Eta on the page to the right. Say the name out loud each time you write the letter.

2 Underline the Etas in the following Greek lines and sentences.

Η ΚΑΙΝΗ ΔΙΑΘΗΚΗ

John 1:21-23 και ηρωτησαν αυτον, Τι ουν; Ηλιας ει συ; και λεγει, Ουκ ειμι. Ο προφητης ει συ; και απεκριθη, Ου. ειπον ουν αυτω, Τις ει; ινα αποκρισιν δωμεν τοις πεμψασιν ημας· ... εφη, Εγω φωνη βοωντος εν τη ερημω, Ευθυνατε την οδον Κυριου· καθως ειπεν Ησαιας ο προφητης.

The sound of Eta is like the sound of the English letters EY in whey.

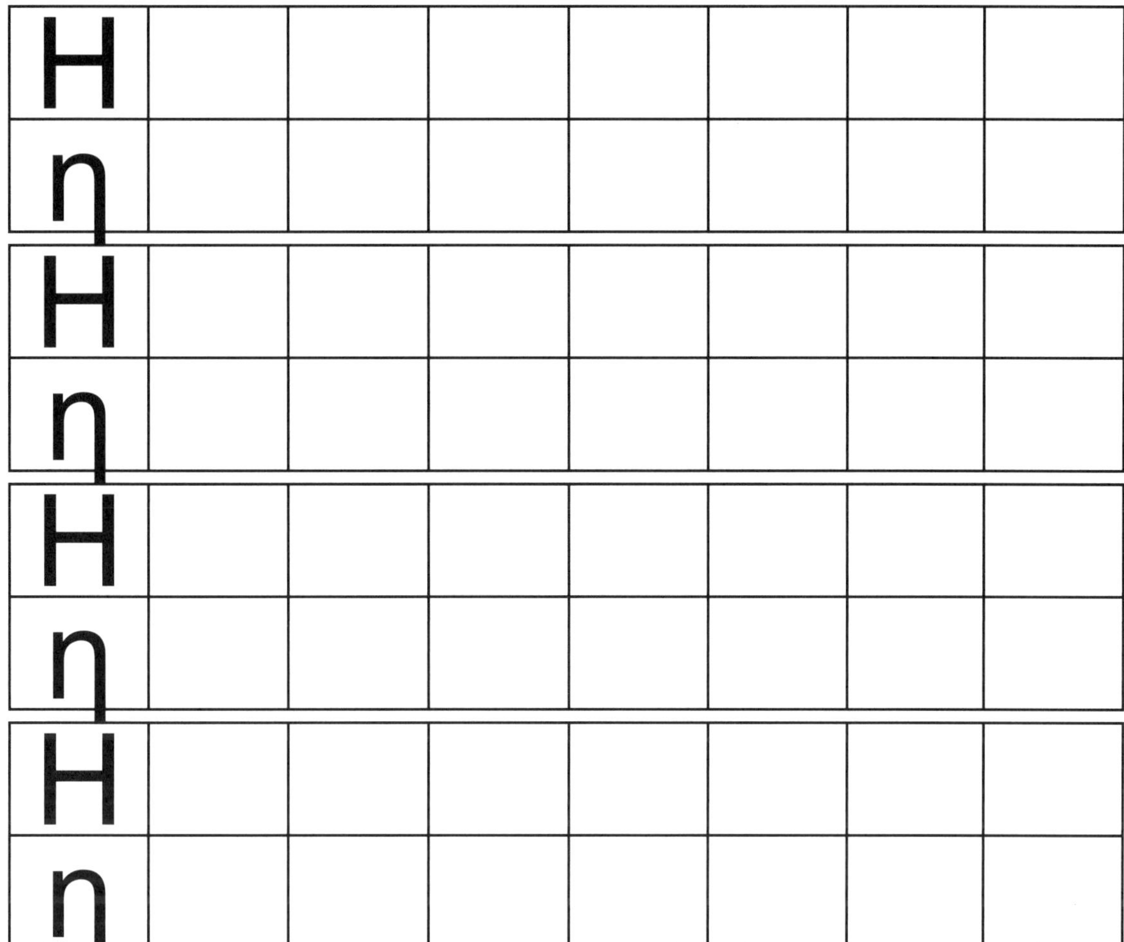

3 In the following sentences, underline the English letters which sound like Eta.

Example: ob<u>ey</u> w<u>ai</u>t

Gail paid her way into the matinee.

Kate takes eight cakes to the cafe.

The valet wore a suede breaker.

The station has a pressure gauge.

Abe feigned that he had fainted.

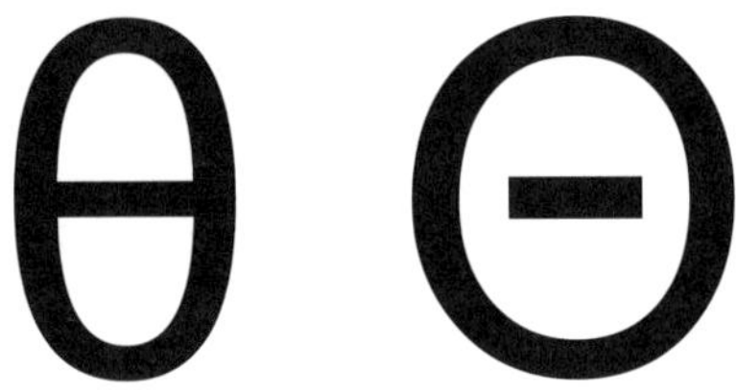

This letter is called Theta (as in "Edi<u>th āte ä</u>ll").

1 Practice writing capital and lowercase Theta on the page to the right. Say the name out loud each time you write the letter.

2 Underline the Thetas in the following Greek lines and sentences.

John 9:30,31 απεκριθη ο ανθρωπος και ειπεν αυτοις, εν γαρ τουτω θαυμαστον εστιν, οτι υμεις ουκ οιδατε ποθεν εστι, και ανεωξε μου τους οφθαλμους. οιδαμεν δε οτι αμαρτωλων ο Θεος ουκ ακουει· αλλ εαν τις θεοσεβης η, και το θελημα αυτου ποιη, τουτου ακουει.

The sound of Theta is like the sound of the English letters TH in <u>th</u>in (not as in <u>th</u>en).

Θ							
θ							
Θ							
θ							
Θ							
θ							
Θ							
θ							

3 In the following sentences, underline the English letters which sound like Theta.
Example: bath myth

If through thick, then through thin.
Thomas bathed in a lathered bath.
His asthma thwarts his breathing.
Threshers threaten to throw thorns.
Ethan thought it through.

ι Ι

This letter is called Iota (as in "W<u>ē ōwe Tŏ</u>dd").

1 Practice writing capital and lowercase Iota on the page to the right. Say the name out loud each time you write the letter.

2 Underline the Iotas in the following Greek lines and sentences.

John 1:19-20 Και αυτη εστιν η μαρτυρια του Ιωαννου, οτε απεστειλαν οι Ιουδαιοι εξ Ιεροσολυμων ιερεις και Λευιτας, ινα ερωτησωσιν αυτον, Συ τις ει; και ωμολογησε, και ουκ ηρνησατο· και ωμολογησεν, Οτι ουκ ειμι εγω ο Χριστος.

The sound of Iota is like the sound of the English letter I in ch<u>i</u>n.

3 In the following sentences, underline the English letters which sound like Iota. Example: w<u>i</u>n my<u>y</u>th

Flynn flies with wings spread wide.
The king signs the English writ.
The sieve is built to catch insects.
Women inhabit fields and cities.
I am chilly, but this chili is hot.

Greek vowel sounds may be *short* or *long*. The sound of *short* Iota is like the sound of the English letter I in chin. The sound of *long* Iota is like the sound of the English letter I in machine. The sound in machine lasts a little longer than the sound in chin.

In English, we commonly indicate the *long* sound of Iota by what we call the long "E" sound in sheen. Many European languages actually assign this English long "E" sound to the vowel symbol I. So English is a little out of step with European languages on the pronunciation of some vowel letters.

4 In the following list of English words, underline the letters which sound like Iota – whether long or short – then draw an additional *macron* ¯ over the letters which represent the *long* sound of Iota. Example: tint mēān

fit forfeit live sieve intrigue prairie irritate eerie fee kit biscuit kilt built

sing England magazine debris key
win women minty myth field chief

You may assume that all Iotas in this book are to be pronounced short unless we show you otherwise with a macron (ī) over the letter.

Whenever Iota is followed by another vowel, it has the consonantal "Y" sound of I in savior (compare royal). In English, when we pronounce certain sounds together, we form a "Y" sound between the letters: dial is pronounced dī-yal.

5 In the following list of English words, underline the letters which represent the "Y" sound, or produce the "Y" sound between the letters, like the consonantal Iota. Example: your savior dial

yo-yo brilliant tortilla hallelujah
yield dial diet companion
you ewe yews use Jews juice
hue hew Hugh unit eunuch

An Iota *Subscript* is a miniature Iota which is placed underneath three long vowels: Alpha (ᾳ), Eta (ῃ), and another long vowel letter which we will learn later. When Alpha or Eta are capitalized, then this Iota is written after the capital as a miniature *Adscript* (Aι Hι), although some moden fonts have introduced a capital *Subscript* (ᾼ ῌ).

6 Practice writing Iota Subscript and Iota Adscript on the page to the right. Say "Iota Subscript" or "Iota Adscript" out loud each time you write the letter.

Iota Subscript is usually considered to be silent, like the silent I in cha<u>i</u>n. We will consider later another option for the pronunciation of Iota Subscript or Iota Adscript, but for now we will consider them to be silent.

So the sounds of Iota are like the sounds of the English letter I in ch<u>i</u>n (short), or in mach<u>i</u>ne (long), or the consonantal "Y" sound in sav<u>i</u>or, or considered silent as in cha<u>i</u>n.

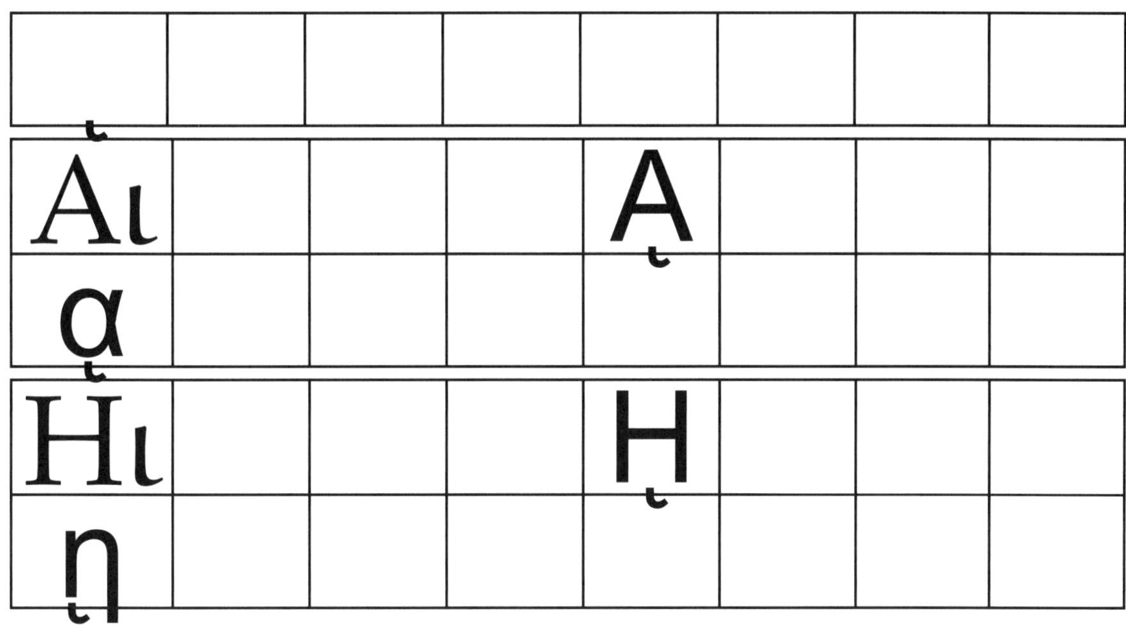

7 In the following list of English words, underline the letters which represent one of the four sounds of Iota. Example: chistle cheese onion wait

is easel yeast easily Italy Spain
icing icy idea idiom Indian
Indiana Illinois easy radii yield
ignite nightly lying field real

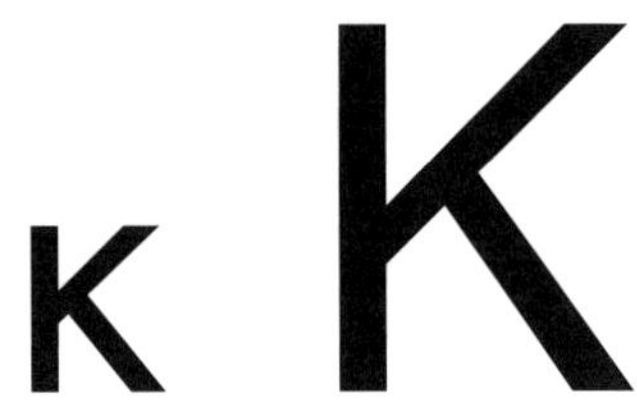

This letter is called Kappa (as in "cŏp ŏn").

1 Practice writing capital and lowercase Kappa on the page to the right. Say the name out loud each time you write the letter.

2 Underline the Kappas in the following Greek lines and sentences.

Η ΚΑΙΝΗ ΔΙΑΘΗΚΗ

John 20:15-16 λεγει αυτη ο Ιησους, γυναι, τι κλαιεις; τινα ζητεις; εκεινη δοκουσα οτι ο κηπουρος εστι, λεγει αυτω, Κυριε, ει συ εβαστασας αυτον, ειπε μοι που αυτον εθηκας· καγω αυτον αρω. λεγει αυτη ο Ιησους, Μαρια. στραφεισα εκεινη λεγει αυτω, ραββουνι· ο λεγεται, διδασκαλε.

The sound of Kappa is like the sound of the English letters K or CK in kicker.

Κ							
κ							
Κ							
κ							
Κ							
κ							
Κ							
κ							

3 In the following sentences, underline the English letters which sound like Kappa.
Example: crack milk

Kent cracked the criminal case.
Karen knocked at the closed door.
The lacquer on the car is unique.
Send a bouquet to each chorus.
The chandelier shocked Jacques.

This letter is called Lambda (as in "Isläm dŏt").

1 Practice writing capital and lowercase Lambda on the page to the right. Say the name out loud each time you write the letter.

2 Underline the Lambdas in the following Greek lines and sentences.

John 12:9-11 εγνω ουν οχλος πολυς εκ των Ιουδαιων οτι εκει εστι· και ηλθον ου δια τον Ιησουν μονον, αλλ ινα και τον Λαζαρον ιδωσιν, ον ηγειρεν εκ νεκρων. εβουλευσαντο δε οι αρχιερεις, ινα και τον Λαζαρον αποκτεινωσιν· οτι πολλοι δι αυτον υπηγον των Ιουδαιων, και επιστευον εις τον Ιησουν.

The sound of Lambda is like the sound of the English letter L in lull.

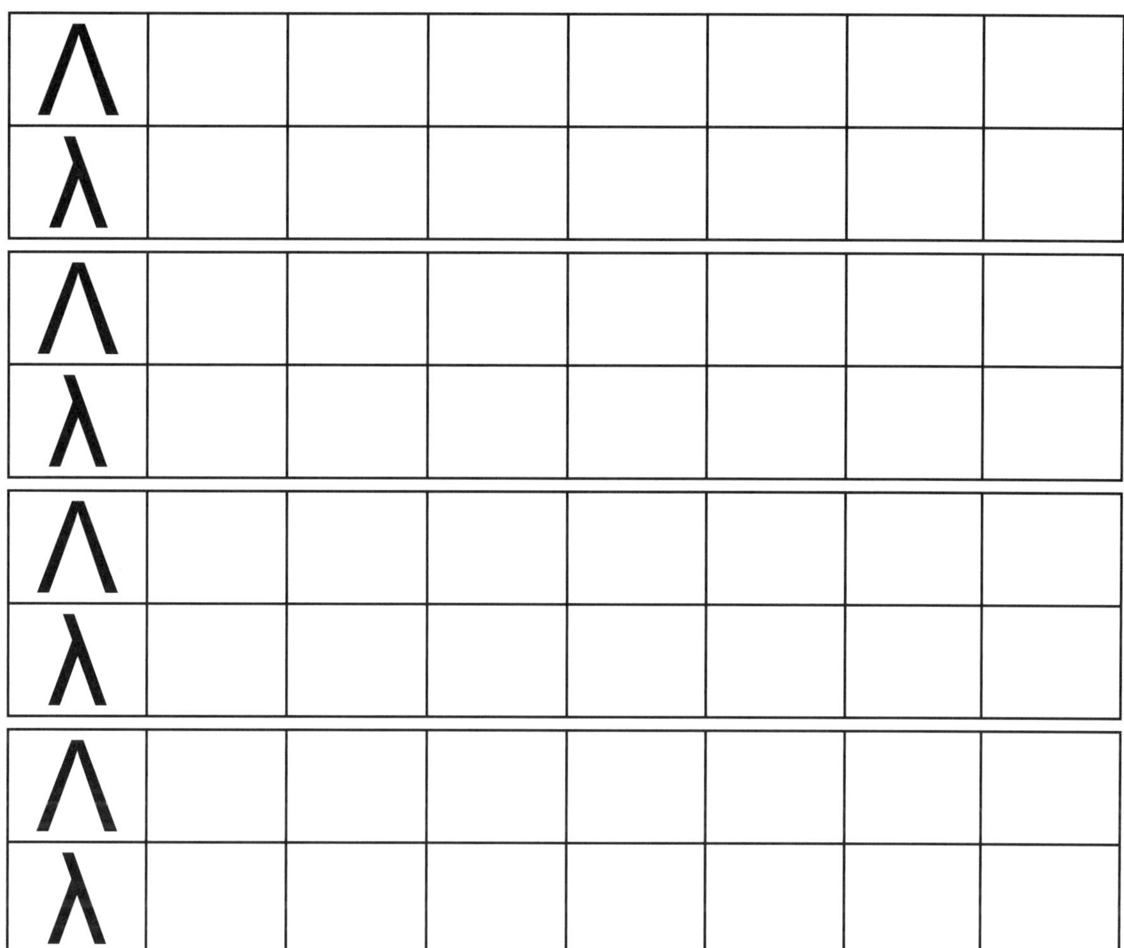

3 In the following sentences, underline the English letters which sound like Lambda.
Example: little ill

Lars believes the flowers are lilies.
Laura flattened a flour tortilla.
Abel was able to label the table.
Sherlock Holmes sure lock homes!
The gorilla climbed the palm tree.

1 Write the English name for each Greek letter and write its lowercase form.

Z	Zeta	ζ
H		
Θ		
I		
K		
Λ		

2 Underline the letters in the English words on the right which represent the sound (or sounds) of the Greek letter to its left.

ζ – adze ads jazz ritzy lens lends
η – cafe debate matinee valet hey
θ – thin hothouse then Beethoven
ι – chili ivy savior debris alibi
κ – click knock city accent accord
λ – lily talk gorilla tortilla calf

The vowel Eta (η) is actually the long of the vowel Epsilon (ε). So now we have three pairs of short and long vowels:

short Alpha — Ă ᾰ — yacht
long Alpha — Ā ᾱ — yawn

short Epsilon — Ε ε — whet
long Eta — Η η — whey

short Iota — Ĭ ῐ — chin
long Iota — Ī ῑ — machine

Iota also has the consonantal glide "Y" sound when followed by another vowel, and the silent Subscript or Adscript:

Iota Glide — savior
Iota Subscript/Adscript — chain

Gamma also has a Nasal sound when followed by a Palatal consonant like Gamma or Kappa:
sinking

There will only be a couple more Greek letters which may represent more than one sound.

3 Write the number of the Greek phonetic spelling on the left which matches the English word on the right.

0. λῑκ ———————— _0_ leak
1. βλῐγκ __ keel
2. ηκ __ blades
3. κῐζ __ bids
4. λῐκ __ lay
5. βαλδ __ bleed
6. κλῑκ __ ale
7. βλακ __ dolled
8. κη __ link
9. ληκ __ blink
10. καλδ __ cake
11. λῐζ __ kick
12. δῑλ __ ache
13. βη̯λδ __ ink
14. βληζ __ kids
15. γῐλζ __ think

16. βλῑδ	__ lids
17. βῐλζ	__ lake
18. ῐγκ	__ block
19. λῐγκ	__ clique
20. βῐζ	__ bleak
21. θῐγκ	__ killed
22. κῑλ	__ guilds
23. λη	__ deal
24. δαλδ	__ Kay
25. κῐκ	__ thick
26. κηκ	__ bailed
27. ηλ	__ bald
28. βλῑκ	__ builds
29. κῐλδ	__ called
30. θῐκ	__ lick

μ M

This letter is called Mu (as in "amūse").

1 Practice writing capital and lowercase Mu on the page to the right. Say the name out loud each time you write the letter.

2 Underline the Mus in the following Greek lines and sentences.

John 5:45-47 μη δοκειτε οτι εγω κατηγορησω υμων προς τον πατερα· εστιν ο κατηγορων υμων, Μωσης, εις ον υμεις ηλπικατε. ει γαρ επιστευετε Μωσῃ, επιστευετε αν εμοι· περι γαρ εμου εκεινος εγραψεν. ει δε τοις εκεινου γραμμασιν ου πιστευετε, πως τοις εμοις ρημασι πιστευσετε;

The sound of Mu is like the sound of the English letter M in mom.

Μ							
μ							
Μ							
μ							
Μ							
μ							
Μ							
μ							

3 In the following sentences, underline the English letters which sound like Mu.

Example: member tomb

Mommy mends me when I'm hurt.
A solemn psalm is a humble hymn.
Most members mingle in the mall.
Mnemonic names numb memories.
First comes summer, then autumn.

ν N

This letter is called Nu (as in "new").

1 Practice writing capital and lowercase Nu on the page to the right. Say the name out loud each time you write the letter.

2 Underline the Nus in the following Greek lines and sentences.

John 1:45,46 Ευρισκει Φιλιππος τον Ναθαναηλ, και λεγει αυτῳ, Ον εγραψε Μωσης εν τῳ νομῳ και οι προφηται, ευρηκαμεν, Ιησουν τον υιον του Ιωσηφ τον απο Ναζαρετ. και ειπεν αυτῳ Ναθαναηλ, Εκ Ναζαρετ δυναται τι αγαθον ειναι; λεγει αυτῳ Φιλιππος, Ερχου και ιδε.

The sound of Nu is like the sound of the English letter N in noon.

N							
ν							
N							
ν							
N							
ν							
N							
ν							

3 In the following sentences, underline the English letters which sound like Nu.
Example: nanny not

Annie sang a song that night.
The knight will not untie the knot.
Mnemonic names numb memories.
None knew the new nun.
A blood hound knows by his nose.

This letter is called Ksi (as in "proxy").

1 Practice writing capital and lowercase Ksi on the page to the right. Say the name out loud each time you write the letter.

2 Underline the Ksis in the following Greek lines and sentences.

ΠΡΑΞΕΙΣ ΑΠΟΣΤΟΛΩΝ

John 13:30-32 ... ευθεως εξηλθεν· ην δε νυξ. οτε εξηλθε, λεγει ο Ιησους, νυν εδοξασθη ο υιος του ανθρωπου, και ο Θεος εδοξασθη εν αυτῳ. ει ο Θεος εδοξασθη εν αυτῳ, και ο Θεος δοξασει αυτον εν εαυτῳ, και ευθυς δοξασει αυτον.

The sound of Ksi is like the sound of the English letter X in axe (compare the letters KS or CKS in taks tacks).

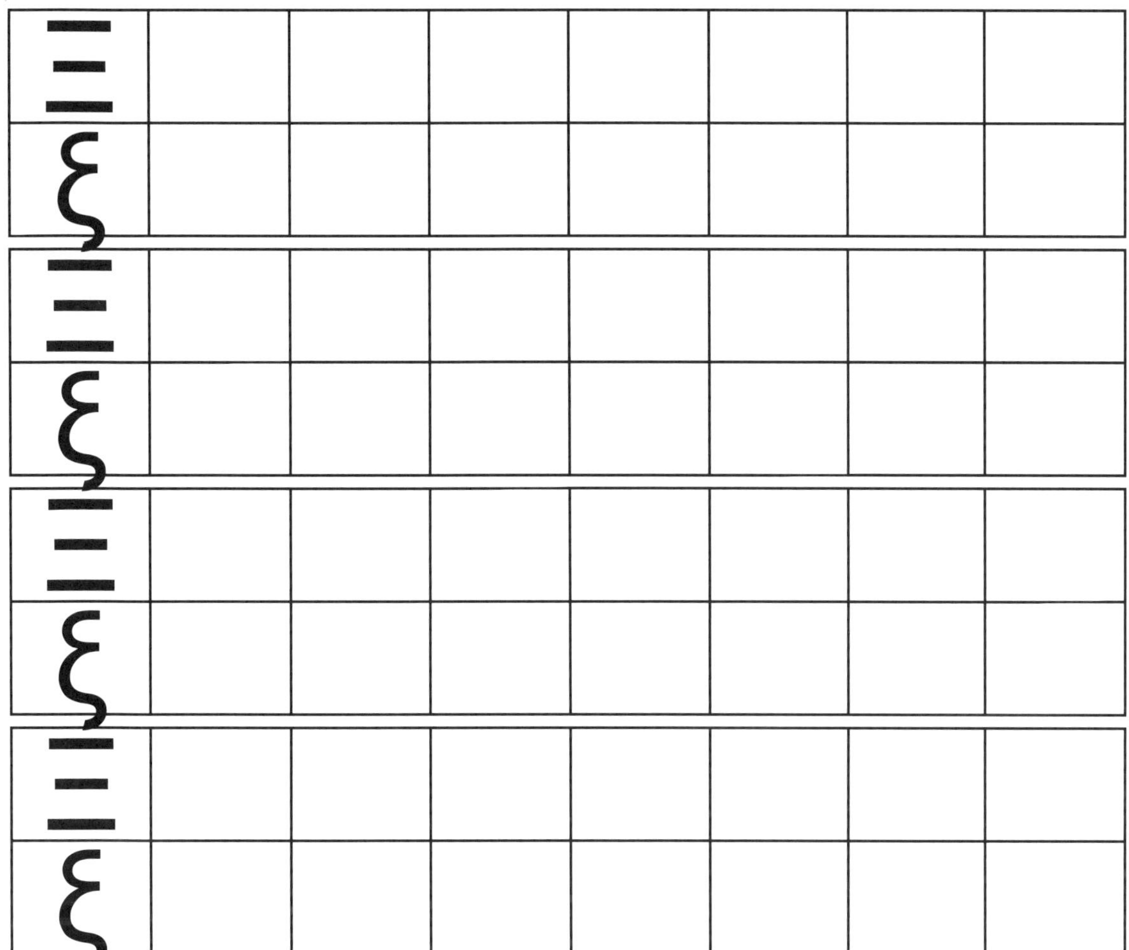

3 In the following sentences, underline the English letters which sound like Ksi.
Example: a<u>x</u>iom Za<u>ch's</u>

Ship decks are in excellent shape.
Jack's jokes are extra eccentric.
Max is ecstatic at the music-stand.
Xerox exact copies of xylophones.
The next fax connects the facts.

ο Ο

This letter is called Omicron (as in "ōh Mĭck rōan").

1 Practice writing capital and lowercase Omicron on the page to the right. Say the name out loud each time you write the letter.

2 Underline the Omicrons in the following Greek lines and sentences.

John 1:16-18 και εκ του πληρωματος αυτου ημεις παντες ελαβομεν και χαριν αντι χαριτος· οτι ο νομος δια Μωσεως εδοθη, η χαρις και η αληθεια δια Ιησου Χριστου εγενετο. Θεον ουδεις εωρακε πωποτε· ο μονογενης υιος, ο ων εις τον κολπον του πατρος, εκεινος εξηγησατο.

The sound of Omicron is like the sound of the English letter O in oh.

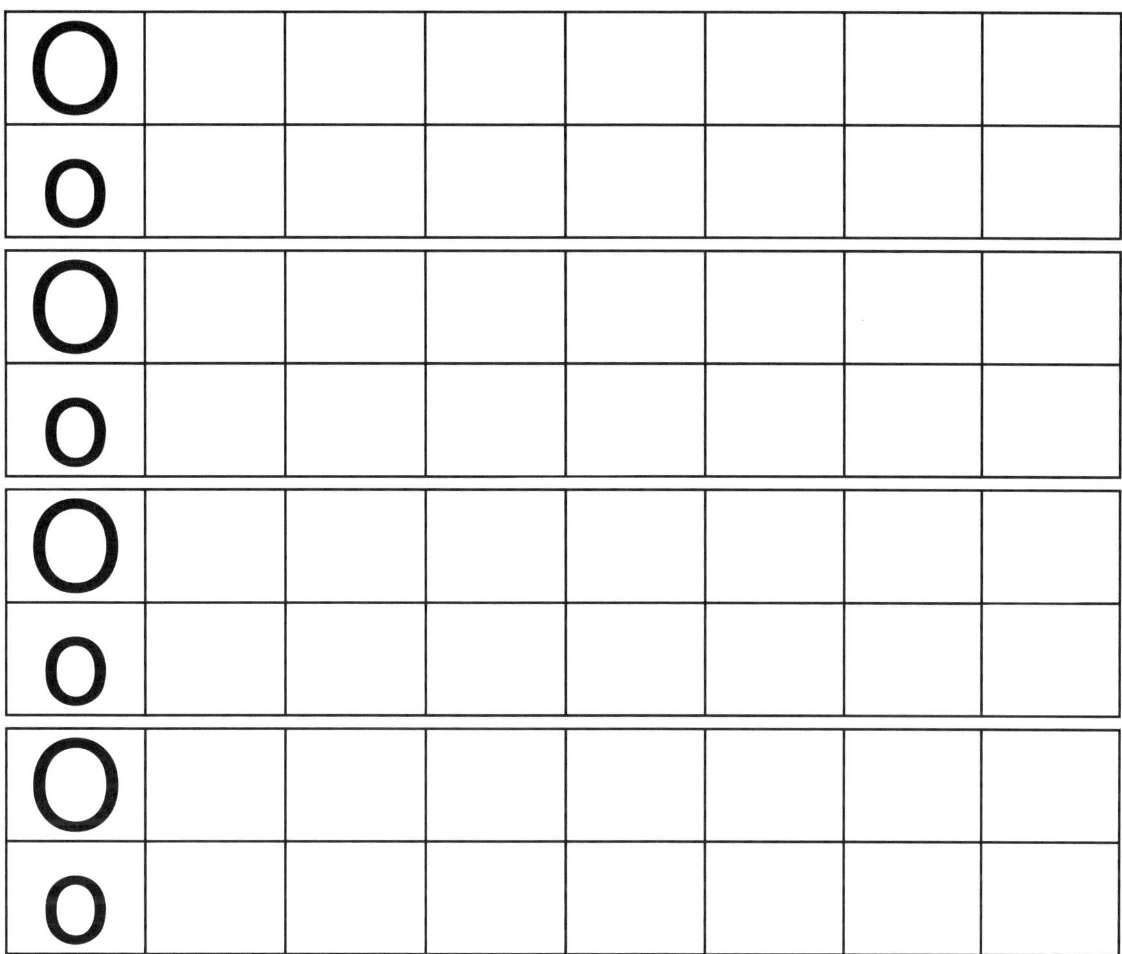

3 In the following sentences, underline the English letters which sound like Omicron.

Example: n<u>o</u>te fl<u>oa</u>t

Otto rode a colt in the rodeo show.

Orey owed only for one doughnut.

Joan wrote, “An Ode to a Toad.”

Otto towed an auto across the road.

Cody knows code for a nose cold.

1 Write the English name for each Greek letter and write its lowercase form.

Μ	Mu	μ
Ν		
Ξ		
Ο		

2 Underline the letters in the English words on the right which represent the sound of the Greek letter to its left.

μ – thumb thimble mommy solemn
ν – inn none gnat knot pneumonia
ξ – fox exacts kicks xerox excel
ο – note not nothing goat depot oh

3 Write the number of the Greek phonetic spelling on the left which matches the English word on the right.

0. νο ——————— _0_ know
1. μῐγξ __ ohm
2. δαξ __ gleam
3. νῑδ __ dame
4. οξ __ blonde
5. θῐγξ __ cane
6. βλενζ __ blinks
7. κῐγξ __ limb
8. μῑκ __ knead
9. ομ __ oaks
10. βολδ __ thinks
11. λῐμ __ docks
12. κην __ kinks
13. γλῑμ __ minks
14. βλανδ __ blends
15. βλῐγξ __ meek
16. δημ __ bold

Almost every Greek word has just one syllable with an accent mark. A few words have no accent mark. Almost no words have two accent marks. The accent mark will appear before a capital vowel (Ά Έ Ή Ί Ό) or above a lowercase vowel (ά έ ή ί ό) or on the second vowel of a vowel pair (αί εί οί). (We will study vowel pairs later.) Iota Subscript is an exception, where the accent mark goes over the first vowel (ῄ).

There are three styles of Greek accent marks. The Acute Accent (´) may appear on any of the last three syllables. The Circumflex Accent (ˆ) may appear on either of the last two syllables, but only over a long vowel or vowel pair. The Grave Accent (`) may appear only on the last syllable. There are special rules for exactly where to place accents. You may consider each accent mark to indicate stress on the syllable where it appears.

4 Practice writing accent marks on the page to the right. Say the name out loud each time you write each accent mark.

From here forward, our examples will include accent marks.

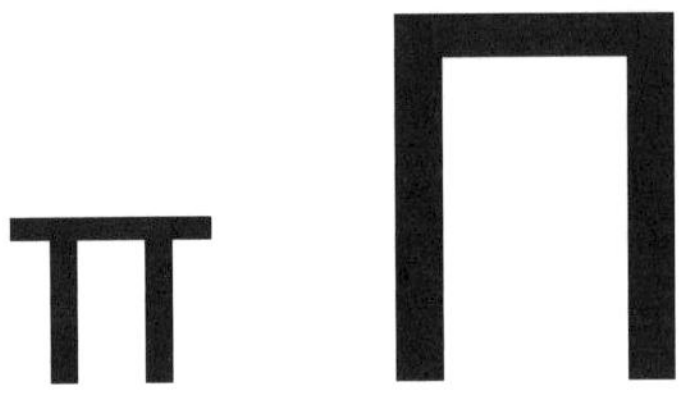

This letter is called Pi (as in "pea").

1 Practice writing capital and lowercase Pi on the page to the right. Say the name out loud each time you write the letter.

2 Underline the Pis in the following Greek lines and sentences.

John 1:32-33 καὶ εμαρτύρησεν Ιωάν-νης λέγων, Ότι τεθέαμαι τὸ Πνεῦμα καταβαῖνον ωσεὶ περιστερὰν εξ ουρανοῦ, καὶ έμεινεν επ αυτόν. καγὼ ουκ ᾔδειν αυτόν· αλλ ο πέμψας με βαπτίζειν εν ύδατι, εκεῖνός μοι εἶπεν, Εφ ὃν ὰν ἴδῃς τὸ Πνεῦμα καταβαῖνον καὶ μένον επ αυτὸν, ουτός εστιν ο βαπτίζων εν Πνεύματι Αγίῳ.

The sound of Pi is like the sound of the English letter P in popper.

Π							
π							
Π							
π							
Π							
π							
Π							
π							

3 In the following sentences, underline the English letters which sound like Pi.

Example: pie top

Perhaps Perry paid for the pastry.
Paul prepared graphs of receipts.
Polly's nephew had pneumonia.
Promptly press pen to paper.
Raspberry pie is in the cupboard.

ϙ Ϙ

This letter is called Qoppa (as in "cōpe päw").

1 Practice writing capital and lowercase Qoppa on the page to the right. Say the name out loud each time you write the letter.

The letter Qoppa was obsolete even in ancient times, but it served a place in the numerical system. Qoppa was used only before the vowel Omicron, and was eventually replaced by Kappa.

ϙόρινθος = Κόρινθος (Corinth)

The sound of Qoppa was like the sound of the English letter Q in liquor. (Compare the letter K in like, or the letters CK in lick.)

2 In the following sentences, underline the English letters which sound like Qoppa. Example: mosquito

Iraq was quick to quash the attack.
Jack sprayed lacquer on the car.
A unique account asks for action.
The chicken crossed the crevasse.
Apples can make a stomach ache.

ρ Ρ

This letter is called Rho (as in "h+rōw").

1 Practice writing capital and lowercase Rho on the page to the right. Say the name out loud each time you write the letter.

2 Underline the Rhos in the following Greek lines and sentences.

John 1:47-49 εἶδεν ο Ιησοῦς τὸν Ναθαναὴλ ερχόμενον πρὸς αὐτὸν, καὶ λέγει περὶ αυτοῦ, Ἰδε ἀληθῶς Ισραηλίτης, εν ᾧ δόλος ουκ έστι. ... απεκρίθη ο Ιησοῦς ..., Πρὸ τοῦ σε Φίλιππον φωνῆσαι, όντα υπὸ τὴν συκῆν εἶδόν σε. απεκρίθη Ναθαναὴλ ..., Ραββὶ, σὺ εἶ ο υιὸς τοῦ Θεοῦ, ... ο βασιλεὺς τοῦ Ισραήλ.

The sound of Rho is like the sound of the English letter R in rhetoric.

Ρ							
ρ							
Ρ							
ρ							
Ρ							
ρ							
Ρ							
ρ							

3 In the following sentences, underline the English letters which sound like Rho. Example: <u>r</u>ow my<u>rrh</u>

Write rhymes in rhythm and meter.
Rhubarb pie is her favorite.
Robert mortgages acres of pasture.
Tigers rarely roam rural areas.
Ruth dresses to impress friends.

This letter is called Sigma (rhymes with "enigma").

1 Practice writing capital and lowercase Sigma on the page to the right. Say the name out loud each time you write the letter.

2 Underline the Sigmas in the following Greek lines and sentences.

John 4:7,9 ἔρχεται γυνὴ εκ τῆς Σαμαρείας αντλῆσαι ύδωρ. λέγει αυτῇ ο Ιησοῦς, δὸς μοι πιεῖν. ... λέγει οῦν αυτῷ η γυνὴ η Σαμαρεῖτις, πῶς σὺ Ιουδαῖος ὢν παρ εμοῦ πιεῖν αιτεῖς, ούσης γυναικὸς Σαμαρείτιδος; ου γὰρ συγχρῶνται Ιουδαῖοι Σαμαρείταις.

The sound of Sigma is like the sound of the English letter S in hi<u>ss</u>.

Σ							
σ							

Σ							
σ							

Σ							
σ							

Σ							
σ							

3 In the following sentences, underline the English letters which sound like Sigma.
Example: ask

Oscar replaced his salt with sugar.
Esther escapes assassin's bullets.
An Hispanic teacher lists six verbs.
Sam locks bats in his safety box.
A special corps insures our safety.

The English letter S actually represents two sounds. In most words, S represents the unvoiced sound, as in ask and hiss. We do not use our vocal cords when we pronounce this "S" sound.

However, when the letter S follows a consonant pronounced by using our vocal cords (such as B, D, G, L, M, N, R), then S often represents the voiced sound, like a Z, as in logs, fads, tabs balls, jams, cans, jars. In a similar way, when Sigma precedes a voiced consonant (such as β, γ, δ) it represents the voiced sound, like a Z, as in Lisbon, Osgood, Esdra.

4 In the following list of English words, underline the English letters which represent the unvoiced "S" sound of Sigma, then place a *caron* ˇ over letters with the voiced "Z" sound of Sigma. Example: sisterš breeže

ease cease sieze as gas goes
this is these thesis debris corps corpse
us husband baptism zippers buzzers

sobs bids sags showers stays
walls slaw gums smug pins snip
slows swells cents sense scents waltz
teas tease measure
pass issue dessert fission

The voiced letters are β, γ, δ, ζ, λ, μ, ν, ρ. (The *GREEK ALPHABETARION* explains which Greek letters represent a voiced sound.) Whenever Sigma precedes these letters, then Sigma represents the voiced "Z" sound.

τ Τ

This letter is called Tau (as in "tŏwn").

1 Practice writing capital and lowercase Tau on the page to the right. Say the name out loud each time you write the letter.

2 Underline the Taus in the following Greek lines and sentences.

John 1:21-23 καὶ ηρώτησαν αυτὸν, Τί οὖν; Ηλίας εἶ σύ; καὶ λέγει, Ουκ ειμί. Ο προφήτης εἶ σύ; καὶ απεκρίθη, Ού. εἶπον οὖν αυτῷ, Τίς εἶ; ίνα απόκρισιν δῶμεν τοῖς πέμψασιν ημᾶς· τί λέγεις περὶ σεαυτοῦ; έφη, Εγὼ φωνὴ βοῶντος εν τῇ ερήμῳ, Ευθύνατε τὴν οδὸν Κυρίου· καθὼς εἶπεν Ησαιας ο προφήτης.

The sound of Tau is like the sound of the English letter T in totter.

T							
T							
T							
T							
T							
T							
T							
T							

3 In thc following scntcnccs, underline the English letters which sound like Tau.

Example: doubt stopped

A thorn stuck into Thomas's beret.
An auto slid straight into the ditch.
In ballet Tara promptly tore her tutu.
The initial question is about a title.
The rain stopped spattering.

υ Υ

This letter is called Upsilon (almost as in "you ōōps ĭll ōwn").

1 Practice writing capital and lowercase Upsilon on the page to the right. Say the name out loud each time you write the letter.

2 Underline the Upsilons in the following Greek lines and sentences.

Matt. 28:19,20 πορευθέντες οῦν μαθητεύσατε πάντα τὰ έθνη, βαπτίζοντες αυτοὺς εις τὸ όνομα τοῦ Πατρὸς καὶ τοῦ Υιοῦ καὶ τοῦ Αγίου Πνεύματος, διδάσκοντες αυτοὺς τηρεῖν πάντα όσα ενετειλάμην υμῖν· ...

The sound of Upsilon is like the sound of the English letter U in put.

Υ							
υ							
Υ							
υ							
Υ							
υ							
Υ							
υ							

3 In the following sentences, underline the English letters which sound like Upsilon.
Example: book would

The woman put her foot through.
A ruined roof would cost too much.
Would a woodchuck chuck wood?
A putter put his dispute to the judge.
Mud on suede shoes is not good.

Greek vowel sounds may be *short* or *long*. The sound of *short* Upsilon is like the sound of the English letter U in put. The sound of *long* Upsilon is like the sound of the English letters UU in vacuum (văk-yōōm). The sound in vacuum lasts a little longer than the sound in put.

*Actually, Upsilon is pronounced more like the German Umlaut. If we pronounced the "EE" sound in beet while we formed our lips to pronounce the "OO" sound in boot, then we would come closer to the sound of Upsilon.

4 In the following list of English words, underline the letters which sound like Upsilon – whether long or short – then draw an additional *macron* ¯ over the letters which represent the *long* sound of Upsilon. Example: book refūse

you ewe yews use Jews juice
young push beautiful continuum

until dutiful culture future guilt
hue hew Hugh humor unit eunuch
coot cute booty beauty putt put pooh
repute fury curious duty bull bugle

You may assume that all Upsilons in this book are to be pronounced short unless we show you otherwise with a macron ῡ over the letter.

We learned earlier that when Iota is followed by another vowel, it has the consonantal sound of Y. In a similar way, whenever Upsilon is followed by another vowel, it has the consonantal sound of W in sweet or U in suite.

5 In the following list of English words, underline the letters which represent or reproduce the "W" sound, like the consonantal Upsilon. Example: suave choir [kwire]

wow sword sway quire toward two
one Juan reservoir suede answer
whole quote write memoir squash

1 Write the English name for each Greek letter and write its lowercase form.

Π	Pi	π
Ϙ		
Ρ		
Σ		
Τ		
Υ		

2 Underline the letters in the English words on the right which represent the sound (or sounds) of the Greek letter to its left.

π – reply cupboard topping graph
ρ – roar carry rhyme write myrrh
σ – cities seize scratches waltzes
τ – title Thomas list listen talked
υ – luck look union suede swayed

3 Write the number of the Greek phonetic spelling on the left which matches the English word on the right.

0. ῡς ———————	_0_ use
1. βαρτ	__ pure
2. πῑς	__ sweet
3. θρῑ	__ star
4. κῐστ	__ grow
5. ροδ	__ Bart
6. βρῠκ	__ sports
7. στρῑτ	__ meat
8. πῡρ	__ rowed
9. σπρῐγ	__ peace
10. συῑτ	__ snoopy
11. μῑτ	__ street
12. σταρ	__ sprig
13. σπορτς	__ kissed
14. σνῡπῑ	__ brook
15. γρο	__ three

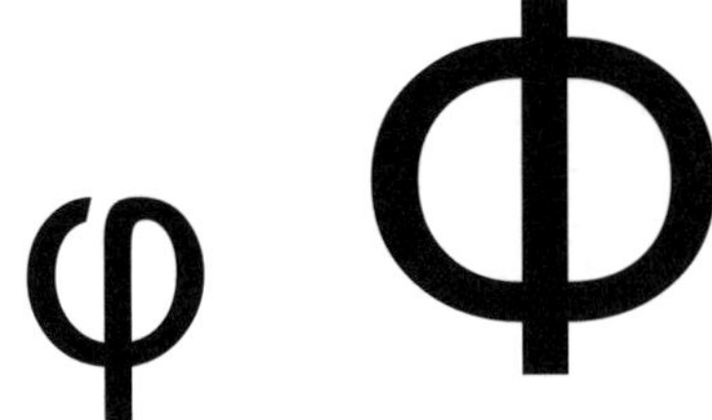

This letter is called Phi (as in "fēe").

1 Practice writing capital and lowercase Phi on the page to the right. Say the name out loud each time you write the letter.

2 Underline the Phis in the following Greek lines and sentences.

... ΠΡΟΣ ΕΦΕΣΙΟΥΣ
... ΠΡΟΣ ΦΙΛΙΠΠΗΣΙΟΥΣ
... ΠΡΟΣ ΦΙΛΗΜΟΝΑ

John 3:29 ο έχων τὴν νύμφην, νυμφίος εστίν· ο δὲ φίλος τοῦ νυμφίου, ο εστηκὼς καὶ ακούων αυτοῦ, χαρᾷ χαίρει διὰ τὴν φωνὴν τοῦ νυμφίου. αύτη οῦν η χαρὰ η εμὴ πεπλήρωται.

The sound of Phi is like the sound of the English letters PH in phosphor.

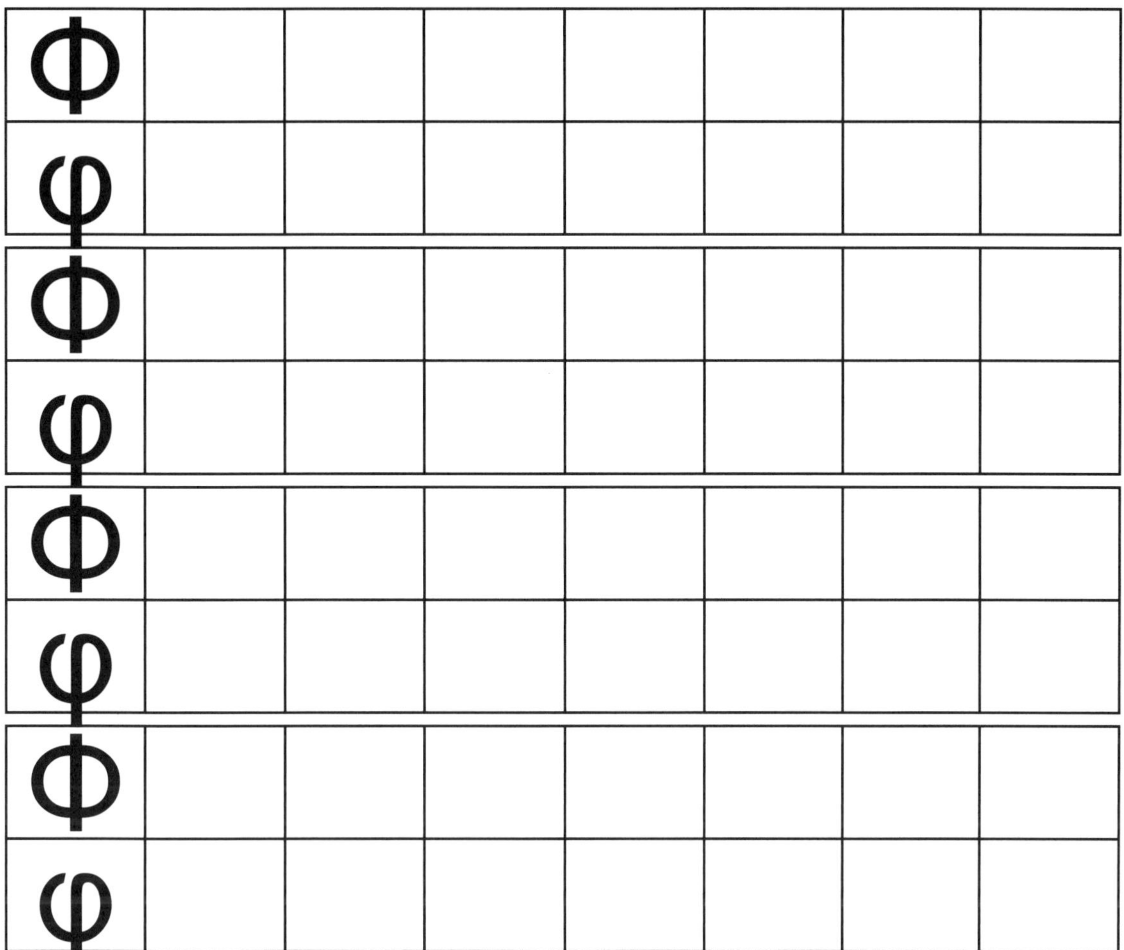

3 In the following sentences, underline the English letters which sound like Phi.
Example: Philip fun

Father favors feathers over fevers.
Farmers put phosphorus on fields.
Fluffy is off to find her furry friends.
Phil has a philosophy on phobias.
Phrases filter through coughs.

This letter is called Khi (as in "lo<u>ch ē</u>ve").

1 Practice writing capital and lowercase Khi on the page to the right. Say the name out loud each time you write the letter.

2 Underline the Khis in the following Greek lines and sentences.

John 7:41-43 άλλοι έλεγον, οῦτός εστιν ο Χριστός. άλλοι δὲ έλεγον, μὴ γὰρ εκ τῆς Γαλιλαίας ο Χριστὸς έρχεται; ουχὶ η γραφὴ εῖπεν, ότι εκ τοῦ σπέρματος Δαβὶδ, καὶ από Βηθ-λεὲμ, ... ο Χριστὸς έρχεται; σχίσμα οῦν εν τῷ όχλῳ εγένετο δι αυτόν.

The sound of Khi is like the sound of the English letters CH in the Scottish word lo<u>ch</u> – a little more raspy than the K sound of the letters CH in <u>ch</u>aracter.

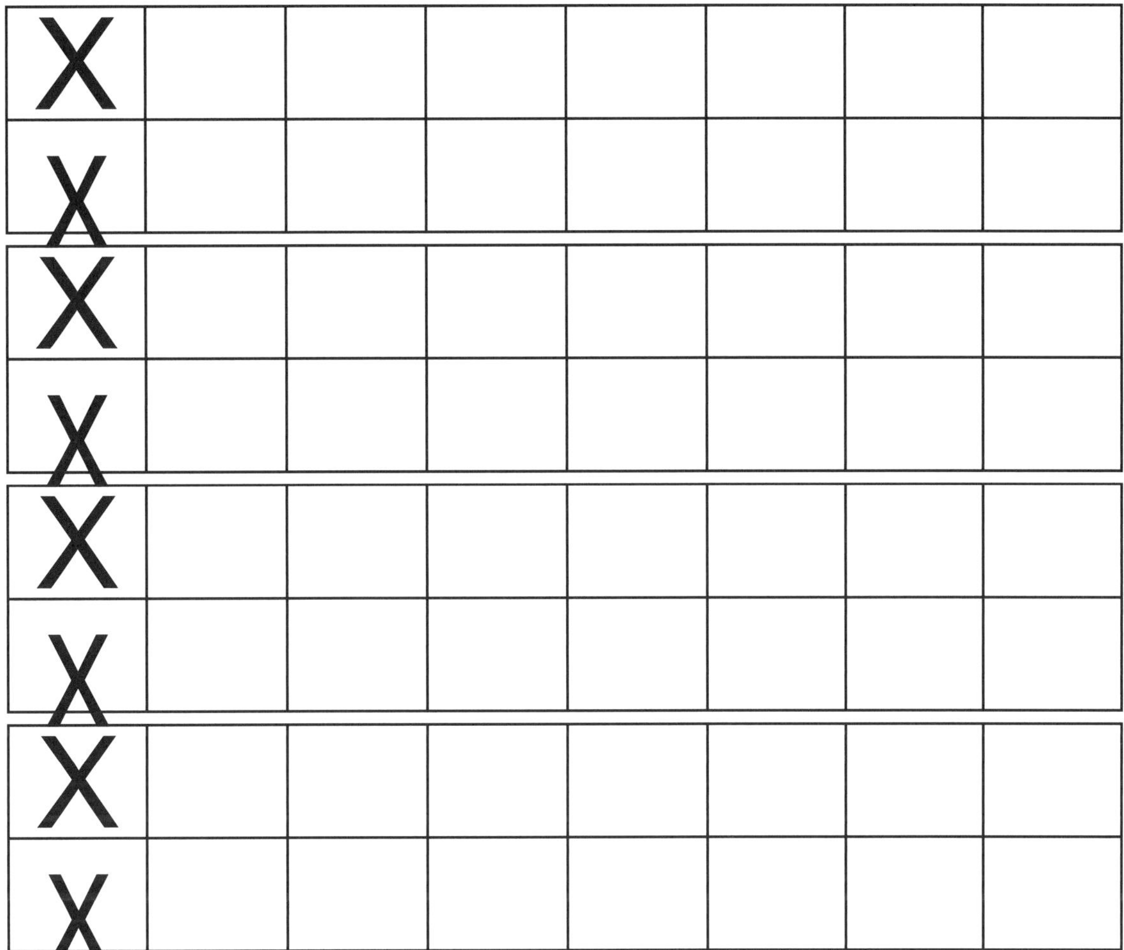

3 In the following sentences, underline the English letters which are close to the sound of Khi. Example: craft Bach

A call echoed across a crevasse.
Kate's stomach felt quite queasy.
The choir sang a child's chorus.
Eric caused a unique accident.
Jack is excited to excavate a cave.

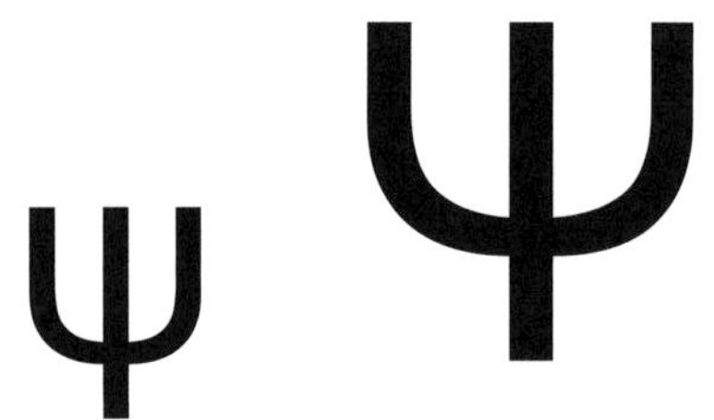

This letter is called Psi (as in "tipsy").

1 Practice writing capital and lowercase Psi on the page to the right. Say the name out loud each time you write the letter.

2 Underline the Psis in the following Greek lines and sentences.

ΑΠΟΚΑΛΥΨΙΣ ΙΩΑΝΝΟΥ

John 13:26-27 αποκρίνεται ο Ιησοῦς, εκεῖνός εστιν ᾧ εγὼ βάψας τὸ ψωμίον επιδώσω. καὶ εμβάψας τὸ ψωμίον, δίδωσιν Ιούδᾳ Σίμωνος Ισκαριώτῃ. καὶ μετὰ τὸ ψωμίον, τότε εισῆλθεν εις εκεῖνον ο Σατανᾶς ....

The sound of Psi is like the sound of the English letters PS in lips, except when it begins a word, when we say only the "S" sound.

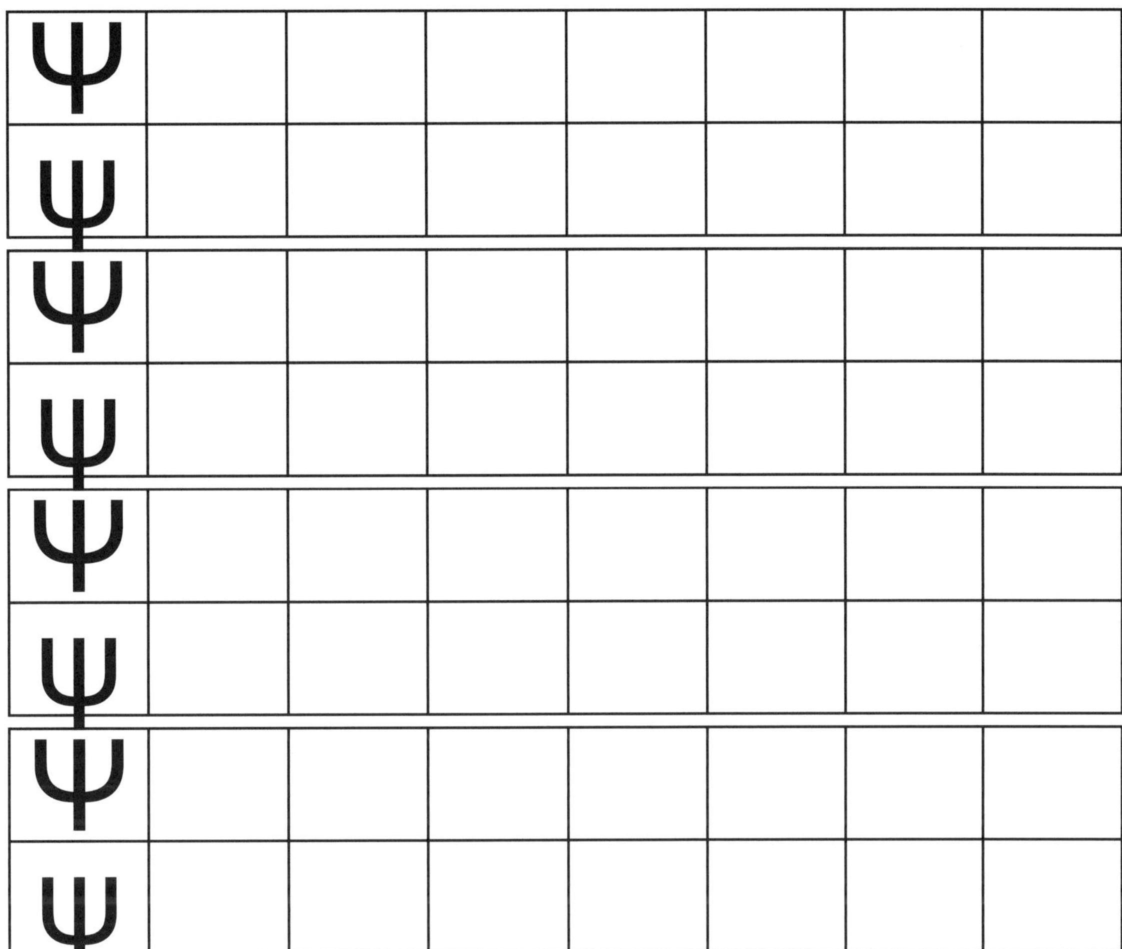

3 In the following sentences, underline the English letters which sound like Psi.

Example: tops popsicle pseudo

I study the psychology of epilepsy.
Flopsy and Mopsy are rabbits.
Sing psalms with sharps and flats.
The army corps buried the corpse.
My pseudonym is Topsy Turvey.

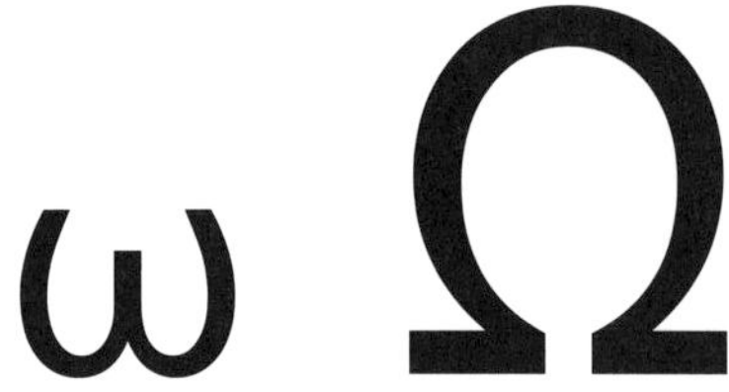

This letter is called Omega (as in "ōwe mĕgäbyte").

1 Practice writing capital and lowercase Omega on the page to the right. Say the name out loud each time you write the letter.

2 Underline the Omegas in the following Greek lines and sentences.

Matthew 1:5 ... Βοὸζ δὲ εγέννησε τὸν Ωβὴδ ....
John 1:9 ἦν τὸ φῶς τὸ αληθινὸν, ὁ φωτίζει πάντα άνθρωπον ερχόμενον εις τὸν κόσμον.

The "O" sound in known lasts a little longer than the "O" sound in note. Omega has the longer lasting "O" sound in known. Omicron has the shorter lasting "O" sound in note.

3 In the following sentences, underline the English letters which we might sometimes

Ω							
ω							
Ω							
ω							
Ω							
ω							
Ω							
ω							

pronounce longer to represent the *long* sound of Omega. (This can sometimes be hard to tell.)
Example: cocoa, homegrown

Otto rode colts in the rodeo show.
Orey owes for doughnut holes.
Joan wrote, "An Ode to a Toad."
Otto tows an auto across the road.
Cody knows nothing of cold cocoa.

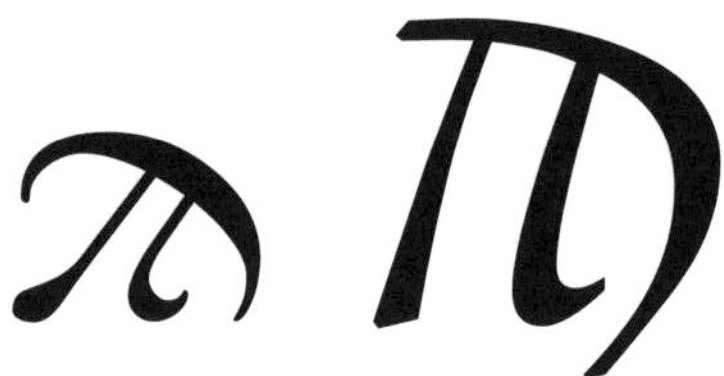

This letter is called Sampi (as in "p<u>sälm pēa</u>").

1 Practice writing capital and lowercase Sampi on the page to the right. Say the name out loud each time you write the letter.

The letter Sampi was obsolete even in ancient times, but it served a place in the numerical system. Its more ancient name is San. The word σαμ-φόρας means "bearing the letter San" – as a horse branded with the letter San or Sampi.

The sound of Sampi is like the sound of the English letters TS in cen<u>ts</u> – the sharper sound of the English letter S in sen<u>s</u>e.

2 In the following sentences, underline the English letters which sound like Sampi. Example: cen<u>ts</u> sen<u>s</u>e.

Fritz accents his consonants.
This counts for dollars and cents.

Π							
π							
Π							
π							
Π							
π							

Prince Samuel sits in his castle.
These prints don’t make sense.
This team puts on the blitz.

‘ ’

These marks are not letters. The left mark is called a *Rough-Breather*. The right mark is called a *Smooth-Breather*.

These marks are placed over vowels, vowel combinations, or the letter Rho whenever they occur at the beginning of a word, and in a few other special places. When an accent appears on the same vowel as a breather, the breather is placed before the Acute or Grave accent (ἄ ἓ), under the Circumflex accent (ἧ ὖ), or to the left of a capital letter (Ἀ Ἑ Ἤ Ἳ Ὦ).

1 Practice writing the Rough- and Smooth-Breather on the page to the right. Say the name out loud each time you write the mark.

2 Underline the vowels with breathers in the following Greek lines and sentences.

John 1:33-34 κἀγὼ οὐκ ᾔδειν αὐτόν· ἀλλ ὁ πέμψας με βαπτίζειν ἐν ὕδατι, ἐκεῖνός μοι εἶπεν, Ἐφ ὅν ἂν ἴδῃς τὸ

Ἁ				Ἀ			
ἁ				ἀ			

Ἕ				Ἒ			
ἕ				ἒ			

Ἧ				Ἦ			
ἧ				ἦ			

Ἱ		ἱ			ἰ		
Ὁ		ὁ			ὀ		
Ῥ		ῥ			ῤ		
Ὑ		ὑ			ὐ		
Ὡ		ὡ			ὠ		

Πνεῦμα καταβαῖνον καὶ μένον ἐπ αὐτὸν, οὗτός ἐστιν ὁ βαπτίζων ἐν Πνεύματι Ἁγίῳ. κἀγὼ ἑώρακα, καὶ μεμαρτύρηκα ὅτι οὗτός ἐστιν ὁ υίὸς τοῦ Θεοῦ.

Whenever a vowel or a vowel blend begins a Greek word, a breather appears over the vowel or over the second vowel of the vowel blend.

Ἀββά Ἁγάρ ἅγιος αἷμα Αἰνών

The sound of the Rough-Breather is like the sound of the English letter H in <u>h</u>air.

3 In the following sentences, underline the English letters which sound like the Rough-Breather. Example: <u>h</u>ello <u>h</u>ay

Hail had hit the whole house.
The jalapeno pepper is hot.
Javier hates gila monsters.

Whenever either Rho (ῥ) or Upsilon (ὑ) begins a word, it always has a Rough-Breather over it.

Ῥαάβ ῥύμη ὕδωρ Ὑμέναιος

The Smooth-Breather is considered silent, like the letter H in <u>h</u>eir.

4 In the following sentences, underline each silent H. Example: <u>h</u>eir a<u>h</u>

Our hour for honesty is here.
He who is humble is heir to honor.
Shepherds annihilate toxic herbs.
Exhort us to exhibit exhilaration.

If our nose is stuffed up by a cold or allergy, we often omit an initial “H” sound from a word. The omission of the sound is often marked by an apostrophe resembling a Smooth-Breather.

Hail had hit the whole house.
’ail ’ad ’it the ’ole ’ouse.

Some Greek texts mark double Rhos with a Smooth- and Rough-Breather (ῤῥ), signifying the rolling of the tongue in pronunciation, like a Scottish rolled “R” sound.

ἄῤῥητος βοῤῥᾶς θαῤῥέω παῤῥησία Σάῤῥα

A breather may occur within a word only when that word is a combination of the word καί (“and”) with another word. This is very rare.

κἀγώ = καὶ + ἐγώ   κἀκεῖ = καί + ἐκεῖ

From here forward, our examples will include breather marks.

1 Write the English name for each Greek letter and write its lowercase form.

Φ	Phi	φ
Χ		
Ψ		
Ω		
Ω		

2 Underline the letters in the English words on the right which represent the sound of the Greek letter to its left.

φ – fife off of phone tuft toughed
χ – chorus kin chandelier candle
ψ – psalm upside corpse corps
ω – stove love board dough owe

3 Write the number of the Greek phonetic spelling on the left which matches the English word on the right.

0. γρηψ ———	0 grapes
1. κλεφτ	__ healed
2. ἡστ	__ bored
3. γρωθ	__ grief
4. θρῐφτ	__ look
5. ῑ̔λδ	__ friend
6. λῠχ	__ loads
7. νων	__ fuel
8. βωρδ	__ haste
9. ποψ	__ thrift
10. ρωζ	__ thief
11. ἁρτ	__ flops
12. γροψ	__ known
13. γρῑφ	__ popes
14. θῑφ	__ cleft
15. φῡλ	__ heart
16. λωζ	__ roads
17. φλαψ	__ growth
18. φρενδ	__ gropes

A COMPLETE REVIEW OF THE GREEK ALPHABET

1 Name and write the three Greek letters which are no longer used in Greek words, but which are still used as Greek numbers.

1. Digamma	F	F
2.		
3.		

2 Name and write the two Greek letters which have more than just a capital and a lowercase form, and write all three forms.

1.			
2.			

3 Name and write the two Greek letters which represent three or more sounds, and give a guide word for each sound.

1.		

1a. ______________________

1b. ______________________

1c. ______________________

1d. ______________________

2.		

2a. ______________________

2b. ______________________

2c. ______________________

4 Name and write the three Greek letters which represent two sounds, and give a guide word for each sound.

1.		

1a. ______________________

1b. ______________________

2.		

2a. ______________________

2b. ______________________

3.		

3a. ______________________

3b. ______________________

5 Name and write the two pairs of Greek letters which actually represent the short and the long of the same vowel, and give a guide word for each sound.

1. (short)		
(long)		

1a. ______________________ (short)
1b. ______________________ (long)

2. (short)		
(long)		

2a. ______________________ (short)
2b. ______________________ (long)

6 Name and write two Greek marks (not letters) which appear over a vowel or vowel pair beginning a word, and give a guide word for each sound.

1.	

1a. ______________________

2.	

2a. ____________________

7

Match the letter symbol on the left with the name and with the pronunciation guide word on the right.

0. β —	0 Beta —	0 bob
1. δ	__ Tau	__ rhetoric
2. ζ	__ Ksi	__ noon
3. θ	__ Pi	__ totter
4. κ	__ Psi	__ dad
5. λ	__ Phi	__ axe
6. μ	__ Dzeta	__ thin
7. ν	__ Rho	__ popper
8. ξ	__ Khi	__ adze
9. π	__ Delta	__ lull
10. ρ	__ Mu	__ kicker
11. τ	__ Theta	__ loch
12. φ	__ Nu	__ lips
13. χ	__ Kappa	__ mom
14. ψ	__ Lambda	__ phosphor

Greek Vowel Combinations

DIPHTHONGS

A pair of vowels which blend together is called a *diphthong* (English pronunciation: dĭf-thông). *Diphthong* is a Greek word (δίφθογγον) which means "dual-voices" or "double-vowels."

In Greek, whenever an accent (´ ˆ `) or a breather (᾿ ῾) belongs over a diphthong, it always appears over the second vowel (αἰ εἱ οί αὺ εῦ οὔ).

PROPER DIPHTHONGS

Proper diphthongs always begin with short vowels – Alpha (ᾰ), Epsilon (ε), or Omicron (ο) – and always end with Iota (ι) or Upsilon (υ).

A *proper* diphthong blends the short sound of the first vowel into the sound of the second vowel.

αι – pronounced äh+ĭh as in <u>ai</u>sle.
ει – pronounced ĕh+ĭh as in <u>ei</u>ght.
οι – pronounced ōh+ĭh as in <u>oi</u>l.
αυ – pronounced äh+ŏŏ as in s<u>au</u>erkr<u>au</u>t.
ευ – pronounced ĕh+ŏŏ as in f<u>eu</u>d.*
ου – pronounced ōh+ŏŏ as in gr<u>ou</u>p.

*Actually, ευ is pronounced more like a toddler who mispronounces the letter L to sound like the letter W, so that f-ĕ-ll (the word *fell*) sounds like f-ĕ-w (not like the word *few*). Since it is difficult for English speaking persons, we'll accept either pronunciation: feud or f-ĕ-w.

1 Underline the letters in the English words on the right which represent the sound of the Greek diphthong to its left.

αι – aisle isle I'll aye eye
sign sigh height buy
lie lye fly

ει – eight ate reign rein rain
veil vale

οι – oil loyal boy buoy

αυ – sauerkraut out doubt crowd

ευ – feud fewed cue view

ου – group fruit to too two through
due dew deuce do dude loop

2 Write the number of the Greek phonetic spelling on the left which matches the English word on the right.

0. αἰ ————————	_0_ eye
1. φοιλδ	__ feuds
2. ναιτ	__ deuce
3. πραιδ	__ how
4. φρουτ	__ baste
5. δαυτ	__ bait
6. φευζ	__ royal
7. δους	__ hewed
8. δαυς	__ food
9. ἁυ	__ foiled
10. φρειδ	__ pride
11. βειτ	__ bite
12. ροιλ	__ fruit
13. φουδ	__ doubt
14. βαιτ	__ night
15. βειστ	__ dowse
16. εὑδ	__ frayed

3 Practice writing accent marks and breather marks over the second letter of the proper diphthongs. Pronounce each diphthong as you write it.

αί			αὶ		
αῖ			αἰ		
εἴ			εἵ		
εἶ			εῖ		
οἱ			οἳ		
οἷ			οἲ		
αὑ			αὓ		
αὗ			αὒ		
εύ			εὺ		
εῦ			εὐ		
οὔ			οὕ		
οὖ			οῦ		

IMPROPER DIPHTHONGS

Improper diphthongs always begin with long vowels – Alpha (ᾱ), Eta (η), or Omega (ω) – and either end with Iota Subscript under a lowercase letter (ᾳ ῃ ῳ – or Adscript with a capital letter Αι Ηι Ωι) or else end with Upsilon (υ).

These are called *improper* diphthongs because a long vowel is already considered to be a double vowel made from two of the same short vowels (ᾱ = ᾰ+ᾰ; η = ε+ε; ῑ = ῐ+ῐ; ω = ο+ο; ῡ = ῠ+ῠ). So these are actually <u>tri</u>phthongs not <u>di</u>phthongs.

> Up to now we have regarded Iota Subscript to be silent. Many grammars drop the sound of the Iota Subscript from these diphthongs, so that the pronunciation of each diphthong is *reduced* to the sound of the long vowel.
>
> ᾳ – is *reduced* to äw as in s<u>aw</u>.
> ῃ – is *reduced* to āy as in ob<u>ey</u>.
> ῳ – *reduced* to ōw as in o<u>we</u>.

The advantage of the *full* pronunciation over the *reduced* pronunciation is that the *full* pronunciation helps us to remember the correct spelling of a word and to distinguish some words which are spelled differently but which would sound the same under the *reduced* pronunciation (Κανᾶ, Κανᾷ; γῆ, γῇ; γνῶ, γνῷ).

When *fully* pronounced, the *improper* diphthong blends the long sound of the first vowel into the sound of the second vowel.

ᾳ – *fully* pronounced äw+ĭh as in saw+it.
ῃ – *fully* pronounced āy+ĭh as in obey+it.
ῳ – *fully* pronounced ōw+ĭh as in owe+it.

1 Write the number of the Greek phonetic spelling on the left which matches the English word or words on the right.

1. κλᾳτ	__ coincide
2. πᾳνσαιδ	__ pay inside
3. κλῃτ	__ claw it
4. πῃνσαιδ	__ hoe it
5. κῳνσαιδ	__ paw inside
6. ῴτ	__ clay it

The last three improper diphthongs (ᾱυ ηυ ωυ) are very rare, and they are always *fully* pronounced – they do not have a *reduced* pronunciation.

ᾱυ – pronounced äw+yoo as in saw+you.

ηυ – pronounced āy+yoo as in obey+you.

ωυ – pronounced ōw+yoo as in owe+you.

Finally, there is one letter combination which is often called a diphthong, but which is actually not a vowel combination at all, but is the consonant glide "W" sound of Upsilon followed by the long "E" sound of long Iota.

υι – pronounced wēē as in suite

2 Write the number of the Greek phonetic spelling on the left which matches the English word or words on the right.

1. στρᾱῡνῑκ	__ wheat
2. αἰωῡ	__ sweetly
3. ηὐ [ῡ]	__ no use
4. πληῡκερ	__ I owe you
5. συιτλῑ	__ straw unique

6. νωῦς __ law union
7. υἱτ __ play euchre
8. λᾱῡιον __ hey you

3

Practice writing the accents and breathers over these seven improper diphthongs. Pronounce each diphthong as you write it.

ᾴ			ᾲ		
αὑ			αὓ		
ᾔ			ᾖ		
ηύ			ηὺ		
αὗ			αὔ		
ᾡ			ᾣ		
ωὔ			ωὕ		
ᾷ			ᾀ		
ωὗ			ωῦ		
ᾕ			ῇ		

Other Vowel Combinations

All other combinations of Greek vowels are pronounced as separate syllables. In English, we can compare this to dividing vowels into syllables in such words as create (cre-ate), deist (de-ist), rodeo (rode-o), linoleum (linole-um).

Occasionally there is a combination of Greek vowels which is spelled like a diphthong (αι ει οι αυ ευ ου ...), but in this particular word the two vowels are pronounced in separate syllables.

When a vowel combination is meant to be pronounced separately, two dots are placed over the the second vowel letter (αϊ εϊ οϊ αϋ εϋ οϋ ...). These two dots are called a *diaeresis* (English pronunciation: dī-ĕr-ĭ-sĭs). *Diaeresis* is a Greek word (διαίρεσις) which means "a dividing into parts." We can compare this to the hyphen we add to the English word co-op to distinguish it from the word coop.

Only the thirteen Greek diphthongs require the accents and breathers to be on the second vowel. All other vowel combinations require the diaeresis to fall on the second vowel of any vowel combination which could be mistaken for a diphthong. The accent mark may fall on either vowel, and the breather mark will always fall on the first vowel when it begins a word.

1 Practice writing the accents, breathers, and diaereses over these various vowel combinations–none are diphthongs. Pronounce each vowel combination as you write it. Notice the relation of the diaeresis and the accent.

αϊ			αΐ		
ἀϋ			ἁΰ		
ἀό			ἁὲ		
ἠῗ			ήϋ		
εΰ			ἀῶ		
ὑΐ			ὤϋ		
ὠΐ			ῶϊ		

A REVIEW OF ALL VOWEL COMBINATIONS

1 Draw a line through each vowel combination which cannot be a proper or improper diphthong.

αε ωα ιο εα ευ αο ωω υη ιε αα ῃ ιυ
οω ιη υα εω ωυ υυ ωο ηω αη υο ει
αω ιω ηη οι αυ υω ωε ου εη ῳ οα
οο εο αι ᾳ ηα εε ηε ιι ωη ηο ηυ ια οε
υι οη υε

2 Place a diaeresis over each vowel combination which requires a diaresis to keep it from being taken for a diphthong.

αε ωα ιο εα ευ αο ωω υη ιε αα ηι ιυ
οω ιη υα εω ωυ υυ ωο ηω αη υο ει
αω ιω ηη οι αυ υω ωε ου εη ωι οα
οο εο αι ᾳ ηα εε ηε ιι ωη ηο ηυ ια οε
υι οη υε

3 Write the number of the Greek phonetic spelling on the left which matches the English word or words on the right.

1. σαιτ
2. κραυτ
3. κρειτ
4. φευδλ
5. ρυϊνδ
6. οἱλ
7. γρου
8. σᾳτ
9. νᾱυ
10. σῃτ
11. ὐηυνιτ
12. ᾠτ
13. νωυ
14. υἱλ

__ gnaw you
__ know you
__ grew
__ wheel
__ saw it
__ weigh unit
__ owe it
__ kraut
__ say it
__ crate
__ feudal
__ ruined
__ sight
__ Hoyle

Chrestomathy

Copy each Greek phrase on the lines below each phrase. Say each Greek word out loud as you write it. The English translation is below each Greek word, with superscript numbers to indicate the English word order.

GENESIS 1:1

Ἐν	ἀρχῇ	ἐποίησεν	ὁ	Θεὸς
In	*(the)-beginning*	*[2]made*		*[1]God*

τὸν	οὐρανὸν	καὶ	τὴν	γῆν.
the	*heaven*	*and*	*the*	*earth.*

JOHN 1:1-3

Ἐν	ἀρχῇ	ἦν	ὁ	λόγος,
In	*(the)-beginning*	*was*	*The*	*Word,*

καὶ	ὁ	λόγος	ἦν	πρὸς	τὸν	Θεὸν,

and-so This Word was immediately-with God,

καὶ	Θεὸς	ἦν	ὁ	λόγος.

and-so [4]God. [3]was [1]This [2]Word

οὗτος	ἦν	ἐν	ἀρχῇ

This-(Same-Person) was in (the)-beginning

πρὸς	τὸν	Θεόν.

immediately-with God.

Πάντα	δι᾽ *	αὐτοῦ	ἐγένετο,

All-(things) [2]*through* [3]*Him,* [1]*have-come-into-being*

* What looks like a Smooth-Breather (’) is actually a Greek apostrophe.

καὶ	χωρὶς	αὐτοῦ	ἐγένετο

and *apart-from* *Him.* [3]*has-come-into-being*

οὐδὲ	ἓν	ὅ	γέγονεν.

[1]*not-even* [2]*one-thing* [4]*which* [5]*has-(ever)-come-into-being*

JOHN 14:6

λέγει	αὐτῷ	ὁ	Ἰησοῦς,

[2]*tells* [3]*him,* [1]*Jesus*

ἐγώ	εἰμι	ἡ	ὁδὸς

"I-Myself am the Way,

καὶ	ἡ	ἀλήθεια	καὶ	ἡ	ζωή· *

and the Truth, and the Life,

* What looks like a raised period (·) is actually a Greek colon or semicolon.

οὐδεὶς	ἔρχεται	πρὸς	τὸν	πατέρα,

No-one comes directly-to the Father,

εἰ	μὴ	δι᾽	ἐμοῦ.

except through Me-(alone).

MATTHEW 5:3-10

μακάριοι	οἱ	πτωχοὶ	τῷ	πνεύματι·

Blessed (are) those (who are) poverty-stricken as-to-spirit,

ὅτι	αὐτῶν	ἐστὶ

because theirs (alone) is

ἡ	βασιλεία	τῶν	οὐρανῶν.

the kingdom of-the-heavens.

μακάριοι	οἱ	πενθοῦντες·

Blessed (are) those (who are) mourning,

ὅτι	αὐτοὶ	παρακληθήσονται.

because they-themselves (alone) will-receive-comfort.

μακάριοι	οἱ	πρᾳεῖς·

Blessed (are) those (who are) self-restrained,

ὅτι	αὐτοὶ	κληρονομήσουσι

because they-themselves (alone) will-inherit

τὴν	γῆν.

the land.

μακάριοι

Blessed (are)

οἱ	πεινῶντες	καὶ	διψῶντες

those (who are) hungering and thirsting

τὴν	δικαιοσύνην·

for-righteousness,

ὅτι	αὐτοὶ	χορτασθήσονται·

because they-themselves (alone) will-receive-satisfaction.

μακάριοι	οἱ	ἐλεήμονες·

Blessed (are) those (who are) merciful,

ὅτι	αὐτοὶ	ἐλεηθήσονται.

because they-themselves (alone) will-be-shown-mercy.

μακάριοι	οἱ	καθαροὶ	τῇ	καρδίᾳ·

Blessed (are) those (who are) pure as-to-heart,

ὅτι	αὐτοὶ	τὸν	Θεὸν	ὄψονται.

because they-themselves (alone) [2]God. [1]will-look-upon

μακάριοι	οἱ	εἰρηνοποιοί·

Blessed (are) those (who are) peacemakers,

ὅτι	αὐτοὶ	υἱοὶ	Θεοῦ	κληθήσονται.

because they-themselves (alone) [2]sons of-God. [1]will-be-called

μακάριοι	οἱ	δεδιωγμένοι

Blessed (are) those (who) have-been-persecuted

ἕνεκεν	δικαιοσύνης·

on-account-of righteousness,

ὅτι	αὐτῶν	ἐστὶ

because theirs (alone) is

ἡ	βασιλεία	τῶν	οὐρανῶν.

the kingdom of-the-heavens.

MATTHEW 7:1-5

μὴ	κρίνετε,

[2]not [1]Do- [3]-continue-sitting-in-judgment,

ἵνα	μὴ	κριθῆτε·

so-that [2]not [1]ye-might- [3]-be-judged,

ἐν	ᾧ	γὰρ	κρίματι	κρίνετε,

[2]with [3]what [1]for (criterion of) judgment ye-judge,

κριθήσεσθε·

ye-shall-be-judged,

καὶ	ἐν	ᾧ	μέτρῳ	μετρεῖτε

and with what (standard of) measure ye-measure-out,

ἀντιμετρηθήσεται	ὑμῖν.

it-shall-be-measured-back to-you.

τί	δὲ	βλέπεις	τὸ	κάρφος

[2]why [1]Furthermore, dost-thou-notice the (tiny)-particle

τὸ	ἐν	τῷ	ὀφθαλμῷ

which (is) in [3]eye,

τοῦ	ἀδελφοῦ	σου,

[2]brother's [1]thy

τὴν	δὲ	ἐν	τῷ	σῷ	ὀφθαλμῷ	δοκὸν

[2]the [1]yet [4](which-is)-in [5]thine-own [6]eye? [3](large-supporting)-beam

οὐ	κατανοεῖς; *

[2]not [1]thou-dost- [3]-consider

* What looks like a semicolon (;) is actually a Greek question mark.

ἢ	πῶς	ἐρεῖς	τῷ	ἀδελφῷ	σου,

Or how shalt-thou-say [1]to- [3]-brother, [2]thy

ἄφες	ἐκβάλω	τὸ	κάρφος

"Permit (that) I-should-remove that particle

ἀπὸ	τοῦ	ὀφθαλμοῦ	σου·

from [2]eye," [1]thine

καὶ	ἰδοὺ,	ἡ	δοκὸς

when behold, that beam (is)

ἐν	τῷ	ὀφθαλμῷ	σου;

in [2]*eye!?* [1]*thine-own*

ὑποκριτὰ,

(Thou) hypocrite!

ἔκβαλε	πρῶτον	τὴν	δοκὸν

[2]*remove* [1]*First that beam*

ἐκ	τοῦ	ὀφθαλμοῦ	σου,

from *[2]eye,* *[1]thine-own*

καὶ	τότε	διαβλέψεις

so-(that) then thou-shalt-see-clearly-(enough)

ἐκβάλειν	τὸ	κάρφος

to-remove that particle

ἐκ	τοῦ	ὀφθαλμοῦ

from *[3]eye.*

τοῦ	ἀδελφοῦ	σου.
[2]brother's		*[1]thy*

MATTHEW 7:12

πάντα	οὖν	ὅσα	ἂν	θέλητε
[2]all-(things)	*[1]Therefore,*	*[3]whatever*		*ye-should-desire*

ἵνα	ποιῶσιν	ὑμῖν	οἱ	ἄνθρωποι,
that	*[2]should-be-doing*	*[3]for-you,*		*[1]men*

οὕτω	καὶ	ὑμεῖς	ποιεῖτε	αὐτοῖς·
in-this-same-manner	*even*	*ye-yourselves*	*be-doing*	*for-them,*

οὗτος	γάρ	ἐστιν

[2]*this* [1]*for* [3]*is*

ὁ	νόμος	καὶ	οἱ	προφῆται.

the Law and the Prophets.

MATTHEW 22:37-40

ὁ	δὲ	Ἰησοῦς	εἶπεν	αὐτῷ,

So Jesus told him,

ἀγαπήσεις	Κύριον

Thou-shalt-love (the)-Lord

τὸν	Θεόν	σου,

[2]*God* [1]*thy*

ἐν	ὅλῃ	τῇ	καρδίᾳ	σου,

with [2]*whole* [3]*heart,* [1]*thy*

καὶ	ἐν	ὅλῃ	τῇ	ψυχῇ	σου,

and *with* [2]*whole* [3]*soul,* [1]*thy*

καὶ	ἐν	ὅλῃ	τῇ	διανοίᾳ	σου.

and *with* [2]*whole* [3]*mind.* [1]*thy*

αὕτη	ἐστὶ

This *is*

πρώτη	καὶ	μεγάλη	ἐντολή.

(the)-first *and* *(the)-great(est)* *commandment.*

δευτέρα	δὲ	ὁμοία	αὐτῇ,

[2]*(a)-second-(commandment)* [1]*Yet* [3]*(is)-like* [4]*it,*

ἀγαπήσεις	τὸν	πλησίον	σου

Thou-shalt-love [2]*neighbor* [1]*thy*

ὡς	σεαυτόν.
as	*thyself.*

ἐν	ταύταις	ταῖς	δυσὶν	ἐντολαῖς
On	*these*		*two*	*commandments*

ὅλος	ὁ	νόμος	καὶ	οἱ	προφῆται
[3]*whole*	[2]*the*	[4]*Law,*	[5]*and*	[6]*the*	[7]*Prophets.*

κρέμανται.
[1]*depend*

SECOND CORINTHIANS 9:6-7

ὁ	σπείρων	φειδομένως,

He-who is-sowing sparingly,

φειδομένως	καὶ	θερίσει·

[4]sparingly; [2]also [1]shall- [3]-reap

καὶ	ὁ	σπείρων	ἐπ᾽	εὐλογίαις,

and he-who is-sowing in blessings,

ἐπ᾽	εὐλογίαις	καὶ	θερίσει.

[4]in [5]blessings; [2]also [1]shall- [3]-reap

ἕκαστος	καθὼς	προαιρεῖται

[2]*each-one* [1]*according-as* [3]*determines-beforehand*

τῇ	καρδίᾳ·

in-(his)- heart (so let him give),

μὴ	ἐκ	λύπης	ἢ	ἐξ	ἀνάγκης·

not out-of emotional-pressure or out-of urgency,

ἱλαρὸν	γὰρ	δότην

[4]*a-joyful* [1]*for* [5]*giver.*

ἀγαπᾷ	ὁ	Θεός.

[3]loves *[2]God*

SECOND CORINTHIANS 13:14

ἡ	χάρις

(May-) the grace

τοῦ	Κυρίου	Ἰησοῦ	Χριστοῦ,

of the *Lord* *Jesus* *Christ,*

καὶ	ἡ	ἀγάπη	τοῦ	Θεοῦ,

and *the* *love* *of-God,*

καὶ	ἡ	κοινωνία

and the communion

τοῦ	Ἁγίου	Πνεύματος

of the Holy Spirit

μετὰ	πάντων	ὑμῶν.	ἀμήν.

(-be) with [2]all. [1]you Amen.

ACTS 21:37

Ἑλληνιστὶ	γινώσκεις;

[2]Greek? [1]Dost-thou-know

Τὰ	Γράμματα	Τοῦ	Ἀλφαβήτου

The *Letters* *of the* *Alphabet*

Α,α	ἄλφα

alpha

Δ,δ	δέλτα

delta

Β,β	βῆτα

beta

Ε,ε	ἒ ψιλόν

epsilon

Γ,γ	γάμμα

gamma

F,F	δίγαμμα

digamma

Ζ,ζ	ζῆτα

dzeta

Κ,κ	κάππα

kappa

Η,η	ἦτα

eta

Λ,λ	λάμβδα

lambda

Θ,θ	θῆτα

theta

Μ,μ	μῦ

mu

Ι,ι	ἰῶτα

iota

Ν,ν	νῦ

nu

Ξ,ξ	ξῖ

ksi

Ρ,ρ	ῥῶ

rho

Ο,ο	ὂ μικρόν

omicron

Σ,σ,ς	σῖγμα

sigma

Π,π	πῖ

pi

Τ,τ	ταῦ

tau

Ϙ,ϙ	κόππα

qoppa

Υ,υ	ὖ ψιλόν

upsilon

Φ,φ	φῖ

phi

ϡ,ϡ	σάμπι

sampi

Χ,χ	χῖ

khi

Ψ,ψ	ψῖ

psi

Ω,ω	ὦ μέγα

omega

Ἀριθμητικά

Numerals

	Ἀπόλυτα	Τακτικά
	Cardinals	*Ordinals*

α′	εἷς, μία, ἕν	πρῶτος
1	*one*	*first*

β′	δύο	δεύτερος
2	*two*	*second*

γ′	τρεῖς, τρία	τρίτος

3 *three* *third*

δ′	τέσσαρες,-ρα	τέταρτος

4 *four* *fourth*

ε′	πέντε	πέμπτος

5 *five* *fifth*

F′ / ς′	ἕξ	ἕκτος

6 *six* *sixth*

ζ′	ἑπτά	ἕβδομος

7 *seven* *seventh*

η′	ὀκτώ	ὄγδοος

8 *eight* *eighth*

θ′	ἐννέα	ἔνατος

9 *nine* *ninth*

ι′	δέκα	δέκατος

10 *ten* *tenth*

ια′	ἕνδεκα	ἑνδέκατος

11 *eleven* *eleventh*

ιβ′	δώδεκα	δωδέκατος

12 *twelve* *twelfth*

ιγ′	δεκατρεῖς	τρεισκαιδέκατος

13 *thirteen* *thirteenth*

ιδ′	δεκατέσσαρες	τεσσαρεσκαιδέκατος

14 *fourteen* *fourteenth*

ιε′	δεκαπέντε	πεντεκαιδέκατος

15 *fifteen* *fifteenth*

ιϜ′ / ις′	δεκαέξ	ἑκκαιδέκατος

16 *sixteen* *sixteenth*

ιζ′	δεκαεπτά	ἑπτακαιδέκατος

17 *seventeen* *seventeenth*

ιη′	δεκαοκτώ	ὀκτωκαιδέκατος

18 *eighteen* *eighteenth*

ιθʹ	δεκαεννέα	ἐννεακαιδέκατος

19 *nineteen* *nineteenth*

κʹ	εἴκοσι(ν)	εἰκοστός

20 *twenty* *twentieth*

καʹ	εἴκοσι εἷς	εἰκοστός πρῶτος

21 *twenty-one* *twenty-first*

κβʹ	εἴκοσι δύο	εἰκοστός δεύτερος

22 *twenty-two* *twenty-second*

κγʹ	εἴκοσι τρεῖς	εἰκοστὸς τρίτος

23 *twenty-three* *twenty-third*

κδʹ	εἴκοσι τέσσαρες	εἰκοστός τέταρτος

24 *twenty-four* *twenty-fourth*

κεʹ	εἰκοσιπέντε	εἰκοστός πέμπτος

25 *twenty-five* *twenty-fifth*

λʹ	τριάκοντα	τριᾱκοστός

30 *thirty* *thirtieth*

μʹ	τεσσαράκοντα	τεσσαρακοστός

40 forty fortieth

νʹ	πεντήκοντα	πεντηκοστός

50 fifty fiftieth

ξʹ	ἑξήκοντα	ἑξηκοστός

60 sixty sixtieth

οʹ	ἑβδομήκοντα	ἑβδομηκοστός

70 seventy seventieth

π′	ὀγδοήκοντα	ὀγδοηκοστός

80 *eighty* *eightieth*

ϙ′	ἐννενήκοντα	ἐννενηκοστός

90 *ninety* *ninetieth*

ϙθ′	ἐννενήκοντα ἐννέα	ἐννενηκοστός ἔννατος

99 *ninety-nine* *ninety-ninth*

ρ′	ἑκατόν	ἑκατοστός

100 *one hundred* *one hundredth*

σʹ	διᾱκόσιοι	διᾱκοσιοστός

200 *two hundred* *two hundredth*

τʹ	τριᾱκόσιοι	τριᾱκοσιοστός

300 *three hundred* *three hundredth*

υʹ	τετρακόσιοι	τετρακοσιοστός

400 *four hundred* *four hundredth*

φʹ	πεντακόσιοι	πεντακοσιοστός

500 *five hundred* *five hundredth*

χ′	ἑξακόσιοι	ἑξακοσιοστός

600 six hundred six hundredth

ψ′	ἑπτακόσιοι	ἑπτακοσιοστός

700 seven hundred seven hundredth

ω′	ὀκτακόσιοι	ὀκτακοσιοστός

800 eight hundred eight hundredth

ϡ′	ἐννεακόσιοι	ἐννεακοσιοστός

900 nine hundred nine hundredth

͵α	χίλιοι	χῑλιοστός

1,000 *one thousand* *one thousandth*

͵β	δισχίλιοι	δισχῑλιοστός

2,000 *two thousand* *two thousandth*

͵ι	μύριοι	μῡριοστός

10,000 *ten thousand* *ten thousandth*

͵κ	δισμύριοι	δισμῡριοστός

20,000 *twenty thousand* *twenty thousandth*

,ρ	ἑκατόν χιλιάδες	δεκακισμῡριοστός

100,000 one hundred thousand one hundred thousandth

ἕκατον μυριάδες	= χιλιάδες χιλιάδων

[1,000,000] one million
(literally: one hundred ten thousands)
= χιλιάδες χιλιάδων *(literally: one thousand (times) one thousand)*

χίλιοι μυριάδες

[10,000,000] ten million
(literally: one thousand ten thousands)

μύριοι μυριάδες

[100,000,000] one hundred million
(literally: ten thousand ten thousands)

Answer Key to Exercises

THE GREEK ALPHABET

Alpha, pages 14-17

2.
John 8:39-40 απεκριθησαν και ειπον αυτω, ο πατηρ ημων Αβρααμ εστι. λεγει αυτοις ο Ιησους, ει τεκνα του Αβρααμ ητε, τα εργα του Αβρααμ εποιειτε αν. νυν δε ζητειτε με αποκτειναι, ανθρωπον ος την αληθειαν υμιν λελαληκα, ην ηκουσα παρα του Θεου· ...

3.
Father called to talk to mama.
They bought tickets for the drama.
Halt in the name of the law.
Her daughter taught her to totter.
Otto ought to audit his autographs.

4.
(Macrons below are only suggested. We aren't very consistent in how long we hold a vowel sound.)
Ānna āria drāma māma
Omahā pāpa banana
catāwba āārdvark lōllipop pōlygon
lāw withdrāwāl dāwdle
squawk scrāwl awkward
ah hurrāh pariah sāhib fāther
alcohol ālmond wālnut fālse tāll talk āll alter
bāll balk bālm fāll asphalt
taught daughter sauce sausage frāud
pāuse vault pāuper pōpper authentic
tot cloth respōnd cōffee brōnze alōng
vōlcano invōlve dōll gōne hōllow sōlid
sōrry bōrrow tomōrrow knōwledge bōmb
Otto ought bought audit odd auto trough
Hārvard carpet carnival departure

Beta, pages 18-19

2.
John 18:39-40 εστι δε συνηθεια υμιν, ινα ενα υμιν απολυσω εν τω πασχα· βουλεσθε ουν υμιν απολυσω τον βασιλεα των Ιουδαιων; εκραυγασαν ουν παλιν παντες, λεγοντες, μη τουτον, αλλα τον Βαραββαν· ην δε ο Βαραββας ληστης.

3.
Caleb wrote the subtle subtitle.
Abbey obviously doubts the story.
Ma Hubbard's cupboard was bare.
Bobby buys baby buggy bumpers.
Below, Blain blows blue balloons.

Gamma, pages 20-23

2.
John 7:51-52 μη ο νομος ημων κρινει τον ανθρωπον, εαν μη ακουση παρ αυτου προτερον, και γνω τι ποιει; απεκριθησαν και ειπον αυτω, μη και συ εκ της Γαλιλαιας ει; ερευνησον και ιδε, οτι προφητης εκ της Γαλιλαιας ουκ εγηγερται.

3.
Gorgeous George grew bigger.
Great green gobs of greasy grime.
A ghost was aghast at the laugh.
He sang as he sank in the sand.
Lang links lynx with lingering lions.

4.
gaggle egg exaggerate [egza-] leggiñgs
binge biñg biñgo bañger añger huñgry
ghost weight ghetto cough aghast through
spaghetti enough sorghum
siñger loñger longitude siñgle
iñk ziñc iñgot liñks lyñx añchor rañcor
give ginger gear range geese
garage gorgeous baggage suggest
negligent diaphragm fragment sign
pregnant engage geography
sañction tañker tangent añxious
leñgth coñquer fuñction distiñct
guess guernsey vogue penguin guild

Delta, pages 24-25

2.
John 6:70-71 απεκριθη αυτοις ο Ιησους, ουκ εγω υμας τους δωδεκα εξελεξαμην, και εξ υμων εις Διαβολος εστιν; ελεγε δε τον Ιουδαν Σιμωνος Ισκαριωτην· ουτος γαρ ημελλεν αυτον παραδιδοναι, εις ων εκ των δωδεκα.

3.
Daddy docks his boat at the deck.
Handsome soldiers [soljers] are doing duty.
The judge [juj] adjourned [ajourn] the jury trial.
The blind man had made fudge [fuj].
We dwell in a dry and arid land.

Epsilon, pages 26-27

2.
John 19:19-20 εγραψε δε και τιτλον ο Πιλατος, και εθηκεν επι του σταυρου· ην δε γεγραμμενον, Ιησους ο Ναζωραιος ο βασιλευς των Ιουδαιων. τουτον ουν τον τιτλον πολλοι ανεγνωσαν των Ιουδαιων ... και ην γεγραμμενον Εβραιστι, Ελληνιστι, Ρωμαιστι.

3.
He exits every [ev-ry] evening [ev-ning] event.
The [Thuh] cafe sold steak and eggs.
Ed decided he called too early.
We cannot guess the next answer.
A video leopard is in jeopardy.

Digamma, pages 28-29

2.
Ϝοῖνος Ϝέργον
Ϝιδεῖν Ϝρήγνυμι
ὠϜόν
ὀϜίς Ϝεαρινός
ἀκοϜή
ἀρόϜω

3.
When will we ever offer enough?
Who were those two suave men?
Wow, what a fine vocal choir.
Juan was one tough fellow.
Very few find what will work.

Review of Alpha – Digamma, pages 30-31

1.

Α	Alpha	α
Β	Beta	β
Γ	Gamma	γ
Δ	Delta	δ
Ε	Epsilon	ε
Ϝ	Digamma	Ϝ

2.
α – all Audrey sad sod bought
β – bill doubt thumb obvious
γ – signal sign sing singe finger
δ – soldier daddy judge handsome
ε – hero head jet evening baked

3.
0. — dog (δαγ)
6. — Bob (βαβ)
10. — ebb (εβ)
8. — egg (εγ)
13. — Deb (δεβ)
9. — daw (δα)
2. — odd (αδ)
11. — Ed (εδ)
3. — dead (δεδ)
4. — bog (βαγ)
14. — beg (βεγ)
5. — gob (γαβ)
1. — baud (βαδ)
15. — bed (βεδ)
12. — daub (δαβ)
7. — God (γαδ)

Dzeta, pages 32-33

2.
Matthew 1:12 ...Σαλαθιηλ δε εγεννησε τον Ζοροβαβελ· Ζοροβαβελ δε εγεννησε τον Αβιουδ· ... Ελιακειμ δε εγεννησε τον Αζωρ· Αζωρ δε εγεννησε τον Σαδωκ· ... Ελιουδ δε εγεννησε τον Ελεαζαρ· Ελεαζαρ δε εγεννησε τον Ματθαν· ...

3.
Unusual floods ruin the foods.
Buds on trees trigger his asthma.
He adds numbers, then divides.
His letter ends in poetic stanzas.
Zelda stands on her hands.

Eta, pages 34-35

2.
Η ΚΑΙΝΗ ΔΙΑΘΗΚΗ
John 1:21-23 και ηρωτησαν αυτον, Τι ουν; Ηλιας ει συ; και λεγει, Ουκ ειμι. Ο προφητης ει συ; και απεκριθη, Ου. ειπον ουν αυτω, Τις ει; ινα αποκρισιν δωμεν τοις πεμψασιν ημας· ... εφη, Εγω φωνη βοωντος εν τη ερημω, Ευθυνατε την οδον Κυριου· καθως ειπεν Ησαιας ο προφητης.

3.
Gail paid her way into the matinee.
Kate takes eight cakes to the cafe.
The valet wore a suede breaker.
The station has a pressure gauge.
Abe feigned that he had fainted.

Theta, pages 36-37

2.
John 9:30,31 απεκριθη ο ανθρωπος και ειπεν αυτοις, εν γαρ τουτω θαυμαστον εστιν, οτι υμεις ουκ οιδατε ποθεν εστι, και ανεῳξε μου τους οφθαλμους. οιδαμεν δε οτι αμαρτωλων ο Θεος ουκ ακουει· αλλ εαν τις θεοσεβης ῃ, και το θελημα αυτου ποιῃ, τουτου ακουει.

3.
If through thick, then through thin.
Thomas bathed in a lathered bath.
His asthma thwarts his breathing.
Threshers threaten to throw thorns.
Ethan thought it through.

Iota, pages 38-43

2.
John 1:19-20 Και αυτη εστιν η μαρτυρια του Ιωαννου, οτε απεστειλαν οι Ιουδαιοι εξ Ιεροσολυμων ιερεις και Λευιτας, ινα ερωτησωσιν αυτον, Συ τις ει; και ωμολογησε, και ουκ ηρνησατο· και ωμολογησεν, Οτι ουκ ειμι εγω ο Χριστος.

3.
Flynn flies with wings spread wide.
The king signs the English writ.
The sieve is built to catch insects.
Women [wih-min] inhabit fields and cities.
I am chilly, but this chili is hot.

4.
fit forfeit live sieve intrīgue prairīē
irritate eerīē [ihr-ee] fēē kit biscuit kilt built
sing England magazīne debrīs kēȳ
win women [wih-min] mintȳ myth fīēld chīēf

5.
yo-yo brilliant tortilla hallelujah
yield dial diet companion
you ewe yews use Jews juice
hue hew Hugh unit eunuch

7.
is easel yeast easily Italy Spain
icing icy idea idiom [i-dee-yum] Indian [in-dee-yun]
Indiana [in-dee-ya-na] Illinois easy radii [ray-dee-yie] yield
ignite nightly lying field real

Kappa, pages 44-45

2.
Η ΚΑΙΝΗ ΔΙΑΘΗΚΗ
John 20:15-16 λεγει αυτη ο Ιησους, γυναι, τι κλαιεις; τινα ζητεις; εκεινη δοκουσα οτι ο κηπουρος εστι, λεγει αυτω, Κυριε, ει συ εβαστασας αυτον, ειπε μοι που αυτον εθηκας· καγω αυτον αρω. λεγει αυτη ο Ιησους, Μαρια. στραφεισα εκεινη λεγει αυτω, ραββουνι· ο λεγεται, διδασκαλε.

3.
Kent cracked the criminal case.
Karen knocked at the closed door.
The lacquer on the car is unique.
Send a bouquet to each chorus.
The chandelier shocked Jacques.

Lambda, pages 46-47

2.
John 12:9-11 εγνω ουν οχλος πολυς εκ των Ιουδαιων οτι εκει εστι· και ηλθον ου δια τον Ιησουν μονον, αλλ ινα και τον Λαζαρον ιδωσιν, ον ηγειρεν εκ νεκρων. εβουλευσαντο δε οι αρχιερεις, ινα και τον Λαζαρον αποκτεινωσιν· οτι πολλοι δι αυτον υπηγον των Ιουδαιων, και επιστευον εις τον Ιησουν.

3.
Lars believes the flowers are lilies.
Laura flattened a flour tortilla.
Abel was able to label the table.
Sherlock Holmes [silent l] sure lock homes!
The gorilla climbed the palm [silent l] tree.

Review of Dzeta – Lambda, pages 48-51

1.

Ζ	Dzeta	ζ
Η	Eta	η
Θ	Theta	θ

Ι	Iota	ι
Κ	Kappa	κ
Λ	Lambda	λ

2.
ζ – adze ads jazz ritzy lens lends
η – cafe debate matinee valet hey
θ – thin hothouse then Beethoven
ι – chili ivy savior debris alibi
κ – click knock city accent accord
λ – lily talk gorilla tortilla calf

3.
0. — leak (λῑκ)
22. — keel (κῑλ)
14. — blades (βληζ)
20. — bids (βῐζ)
23. — lay (λη)
16. — bleed (βλῑδ)
27. — ale (ηλ)
24. — dolled (δαλδ)
19. — link (λῐγκ)
1. — blink (βλῐγκ)
26. — cake (κηκ)
25. — kick (κῐκ)
2. — ache (ηκ)
18. — ink (ῐγκ)
3. — kids (κῐζ)
21. — think (θῐγκ)
11. — lids (λῐζ)
9. — lake (ληκ)
7. — block (βλακ)
6. — clique (κλῑκ)
28. — bleak (βλῑκ)
29. — killed (κῐλδ)
15. — guilds (γῐλζ)
12. — deal (δῑλ)
8. — Kay (κη)
30. — thick (θῐκ)
13. — bailed (βηλδ)
5. — bald (βαλδ)
17. — builds (βῐλζ)
10. — called (καλδ)
4. — lick (λῐκ)

Mu, pages 52-53

2.
John 5:45-47 μη δοκειτε οτι εγω κατηγορησω υμων προς τον πατερα· εστιν ο κατηγορων υμων, Μωσης, εις ον υμεις ηλπικατε. ει γαρ επιστευετε Μωσῃ, επιστευετε αν εμοι· περι γαρ εμου εκεινος εγραψεν. ει δε τοις εκεινου γραμμασιν ου πιστευετε, πως τοις εμοις ρημασι πιστευσετε;

3.
Mommy mends me when I'm hurt.
A solemn psalm is a humble hymn.
Most members mingle in the mall.
Mnemonic names numb memories.
First comes summer, then autumn.

Nu, pages 54-55

2.
John 1:45,46 Ευρισκει Φιλιππος τον Ναθαναηλ, και λεγει αυτῳ, Ον εγραψε Μωσης εν τῳ νομῳ και οι προφηται, ευρηκαμεν, Ιησουν τον υιον του Ιωσηφ τον απο Ναζαρετ. και ειπεν αυτῳ Ναθαναηλ, Εκ Ναζαρετ δυναται τι αγαθον ειναι; λεγει αυτῳ Φιλιππος, Ερχου και ιδε.

3.
Annie sang a song that night.
The knight will not untie the knot.
Mnemonic names numb memories.
None knew the new nun.
A blood hound knows by his nose.

Ksi, pages 56-57

2.
ΠΡΑΞΕΙΣ ΑΠΟΣΤΟΛΩΝ
John 13:30-32 ... ευθεως εξηλθεν· ην δε νυξ. οτε εξηλθε, λεγει ο Ιησους, νυν εδοξασθη ο υιος του ανθρωπου, και ο Θεος εδοξασθη εν αυτῳ. ει ο Θεος εδοξασθη εν αυτῳ, και ο Θεος δοξασει αυτον εν εαυτῳ, και ευθυς δοξασει αυτον.

3.
Ship decks are in excellent shape.
Jack's jokes are extra eccentric.
Max is ecstatic at the music-stand.
Xerox exact copies of xylophones.
The next fax connects the facts.

Omicron, pages 58-59

2.
John 1:16-18 και εκ του πληρωματος αυτου ημεις παντες ελαβομεν και χαριν αντι χαριτος· οτι ο νομος δια Μωσεως εδοθη, η χαρις και η αληθεια δια Ιησου Χριστου εγενετο. Θεον ουδεις εωρακε πωποτε· ο μονογενης υιος, ο ων εις τον κολπον του πατρος, εκεινος εξηγησατο.

3.
Otto rode a colt in the rodeo show.
Orey owed only for one doughnut.
Joan wrote, "An Ode to a Toad."
Otto towed an auto across the road.
Cody knows code for a nose cold.

Review of Mu – Omicron, Accent Marks, pages 60-63

1.

Μ	Mu	μ
Ν	Nu	ν
Ξ	Ksi	ξ
Ο	Omicron	ο

2.
μ – thumb thimble mommy solemn
ν – inn none gnat knot pneumonia
ξ – fox exacts kicks xerox excel
ο – note not nothing goat depot oh

3.
0. — know (νο)
9. — ohm (ομ)
13. — gleam (γλῖμ)

16. — dame (δημ)
14. — blonde (βλανδ)
12. — cane (κην)
15. — blinks (βλῐγξ)
11. — limb (λῐμ)
3. — knead (νῑδ)
4. — oaks (οξ)
5. — thinks (θῐγξ)
2. — docks (δαξ)
7. — kinks (κῐγξ)
1. — minks (μῐγξ)
6. — blends (βλενζ)
8. — meek (μῑκ)
10. — bold (βολδ)

Pi, pages 64-65

2.
John 1:32-33 καὶ εμαρτύρησεν Ιωάννης λέγων, Ότι τεθέαμαι τὸ Πνεῦμα καταβαῖνον ωσεὶ περιστερὰν εξ ουρανοῦ, καὶ έμεινεν επ αυτόν. καγὼ ουκ ᾔδειν αυτόν· αλλ ο πέμψας με βαπτίζειν εν ύδατι, εκεῖνός μοι εἶπεν, Εφ ὃν ἀν ίδῃς τὸ Πνεῦμα καταβαῖνον καὶ μένον επ αυτὸν, ουτός εστιν ο βαπτίζων εν Πνεύματι Αγίῳ.

3.
Perhaps Perry paid for the pastry.
Paul prepared graphs of receipts.
Polly's nephew had pneumonia.
Promptly press pen to paper.
Raspberry pie is in the cupboard.

Qoppa, pages 66-67

2.
Iraq was quick to quash the attack.
Jack sprayed lacquer on the car.
A unique account asks for action.
The chicken crossed the crevasse.
Apples can make a stomach ache.

Rho, pages 68-69

2.
John 1:47-49 εἶδεν ο Ιησοῦς τὸν Ναθαναὴλ ερχόμενον πρὸς αὐτὸν, καὶ λέγει περὶ αυτοῦ, Ἴδε ἀληθῶς Ισραηλίτης, εν ῷ δόλος ουκ έστι. ... απεκρίθη ο Ιησοῦς καὶ εἶπεν αυτῷ, Πρὸ τοῦ σε Φίλιππον φωνῆσαι, όντα υπὸ τὴν συκῆν εἶδόν σε. απεκρίθη Ναθαναὴλ καὶ λέγει αυτῷ, Ραββί, σὺ εἶ ο υιὸς τοῦ Θεοῦ, ... ο βασιλεὺς τοῦ Ισραήλ.

3.
Write rhymes in rhythm and meter.
Rhubarb pie is her favorite.
Robert mortgages acres of pasture.
Tigers rarely roam rural areas.
Ruth dresses to impress friends.

Sigma, pages 70-73

2.
John 4:7,9 έρχεται γυνὴ εκ τῆς Σαμαρείας αντλῆσαι ύδωρ. λέγει αυτῇ ο Ιησοῦς, δὸς μοι πιεῖν. ... λέγει οὖν αυτῷ η γυνὴ η Σαμαρεῖτις, πῶς σὺ Ιουδαῖος ὢν παρ εμοῦ πιεῖν αιτεῖς, ούσης γυναικὸς Σαμαρείτιδος; ου γὰρ συγχρῶνται Ιουδαῖοι Σαμαρείταις.

3.
Oscar replaced his salt with sugar.
Esther escapes assassin's bullets.
An Hispanic teacher lists six verbs.
Sam locks bats in his safety box [boks].
A special corps insures our safety.

4.
eaŝe cease sieẑe aŝ gas goeŝ
this iŝ theŝe thesis debris corps corpse
us huŝband baptiŝm ẑipperŝ buẑẑerŝ
sobŝ bidŝ sagŝ showerŝ stayŝ
wallŝ slaw gumŝ smug pinŝ snip
slowŝ swellŝ cents sense scents waltz
teaŝ teaŝe measure
pass issue deŝŝert fission

Tau, pages 74-75

2.
John 1:21-23 καὶ ηρώτησαν αυτὸν, Τί οῦν; Ηλίας εῖ σύ; καὶ λέγει, Ουκ ειμί. Ο προφήτης εῖ σύ; καὶ απεκρίθη, Ού. εῖπον οῦν αυτῷ, Τίς εῖ; ίνα απόκρισιν δῶμεν τοῖς πέμψασιν ημᾶς· τί λέγεις περὶ σεαυτοῦ; έφη, Εγὼ φωνὴ βοῶντος εν τῇ ερήμῳ, Ευθύνατε τὴν οδὸν Κυρίου· καθὼς εῖπεν Ησαιας ο προφήτης.

3.
A thorn stuck into Thomas's beret.
An auto slid straight into the ditch.
In ballet Tara promptly tore her tutu.
The initial question is about a title.
The rain stopped spattering.

Upsilon, pages 76-79

2.
Matthew 28:19,20 πορευθέντες οῦν μαθητεύσατε πάντα τὰ έθνη, βαπτίζοντες αυτοὺς εις τὸ όνομα τοῦ Πατρὸς καὶ τοῦ Υιοῦ καὶ τοῦ Αγίου Πνεύματος, διδάσκοντες αυτοὺς τηρεῖν πάντα όσα ενετειλάμην υμῖν·

3.
The woman put her foot through.
A ruined roof would cost too much.
Would a woodchuck chuck wood?
A putter put his dispute to the judge.
Mud on suede shoes is not good.

4.
ȳōū ēw̄ē ȳēw̄s ūse Jēw̄s jūīce
young push bēāūtiful continūūm [contin-yoom – or some say contin-yoo-um]
until dūtiful culture fūture guilt
hūē hēw̄ Hūḡh̄ hūmor ūnit ēūnuch
coot cūte booty bēāūty putt put pooh
repūte fūry cūrious duty [dooty] bull būgle

5.
wow sword [sord] sway quire toward [tord] two [too]
one Juan reservoir suede answer [anser]
whole quote write [rite] memoir squash

Review of Pi – Upsilon, pages 80-81

1.

Π	Pi	π
Ϙ	Qoppa	ϙ
Ρ	Rho	ρ
Σ	Sigma	σ,ς
Τ	Tau	τ
Υ	Upsilon	υ

2.
π – reply cupboard topping graph
ρ – roar carry rhyme write myrrh
σ – cities seize scratches waltzes
τ – title Thomas list listen [silent t] talked [talkt]
υ – luck look union suede swayed

3.
0. — use (ῡς)
8. — pure (πῡρ)
10. — sweet (συῑτ)
12. — star (σταρ)
15. — grow (γρο)
1. — Bart (βαρτ)
13. — sports (σπορτς)
11. — meat (μῑτ)
5. — rowed (ροδ)
2. — peace (πῑς)
14. — snoopy (σνῡπῑ)
7. — street (στρῑτ)
9. — sprig (σπρῐγ)
4. — kissed (κῐστ)
6. — brook (βρῠκ)
3. — three (θρῑ)

Phi, pages 82-83

2.
... ΠΡΟΣ ΕΦΕΣΙΟΥΣ
... ΠΡΟΣ ΦΙΛΙΠΠΗΣΙΟΥΣ
... ΠΡΟΣ ΦΙΛΗΜΟΝΑ
John 3:29 ο έχων τὴν νύμφην, νυμφίος εστίν· ο δὲ φίλος τοῦ νυμφίου, ο εστηκὼς καὶ ακούων αυτοῦ, χαρᾷ χαίρει διὰ τὴν φωνὴν τοῦ νυμφίου. αύτη οῦν η χαρὰ η εμὴ πεπλήρωται.

3.
Father favors feathers over fevers.
Farmers put phosphorus on fields.
Fluffy is off to find her furry friends.
Phil has a philosophy on phobias.
Phrases filter through coughs.

Khi, pages 84-85

2.
John 7:41-43 άλλοι έλεγον, οῦτός εστιν ο Χριστός. άλλοι δὲ έλεγον, μὴ γὰρ εκ τῆς Γαλιλαίας ο Χριστὸς έρχεται; ουχὶ η γραφὴ εῖπεν, ότι εκ τοῦ σπέρματος Δαβὶδ, καὶ απὸ Βηθλεὲμ, ... ο Χριστὸς έρχεται; σχίσμα οῦν εν τῷ όχλῳ εγένετο δι αυτόν.

3.
A call echoed across a crevasse.
Kate's stomach felt quite queazy.
The choir sang a child's chorus.
Eric caused a unique accident.
Jack is excited [eksited] to excavate [ekskavate] a cave.

Psi, pages 86-87

2.
ΑΠΟΚΑΛΥΨΙΣ ΙΩΑΝΝΟΥ
John 13:26-27 αποκρίνεται ο Ιησοῦς, εκεῖνός εστιν ῷ εγὼ βάψας τὸ ψωμίον επιδώσω. καὶ εμβάψας τὸ ψωμίον, δίδωσιν Ιούδᾳ Σίμωνος Ισκαριώτῃ. καὶ μετὰ τὸ ψωμίον, τότε εισῆλθεν εις εκεῖνον ο Σατανᾶς ....

3.
I study the psychology of epilepsy.
Flopsy and Mopsy are rabbits.
Sing psalms with sharps and flats.
The army corps buried the corpse.
My pseudonym is Topsy Turvey.

Omega, pages 88-89

2.
Matthew 1:5 ... Βοὸζ δὲ εγέννησε τὸν Ωβὴδ ....
John 1:9 ῆν τὸ φῶς τὸ αληθινὸν, ὸ φωτίζει πάντα άνθρωπον ερχόμενον εις τὸν κόσμον.

3.
(Macrons below are only suggested. We aren't very consistent in how long we hold a vowel sound.)
Otto rode colts in the rodeo show.
Orey owes for doughnut holes.
Joan wrote, "An Ode to a Toad."
Otto tows an auto across the road.
Cody knows nothing of cold cocoa.

Sampi, pages 90-91

2.
Fritz accents his consonants.
This counts for dollars and cents.
Prince Samuel sits in his castle.
These prints don't make sense.
This team puts on the blitz.

Breathers, pages 92-95

2.
John 1:33-34 κἀγὼ οὐκ ᾔδειν αὐτόν· ἀλλ ὁ πέμψας με βαπτίζειν ἐν ὕδατι, ἐκεῖνός μοι εἶπεν, Ἐφ ὅν ἂν ἴδῃς τὸ Πνεῦμα καταβαῖνον καὶ μένον ἐπ αὐτὸν, οὗτός ἐστιν ὁ βαπτίζων ἐν Πνεύματι Ἁγίῳ. κἀγὼ ἑώρακα, καὶ μεμαρτύρηκα ὅτι οὗτός ἐστιν ὁ υἱὸς τοῦ Θεοῦ.

3.
Hail had hit the whole house.
The jalapeno pepper is hot.
Javier [Ha-vee-air] hates gila [heela] monsters.

4.
Our hour for honesty is here.
He who is humble is heir to honor.
Shepherds annihilate toxic herbs.
Exhort us to exhibit exhilaration.

Review of Phi – Sampi, Breathers, pages 96-97

1.

Φ	Phi	φ
Χ	Khi	χ
Ψ	Psi	ψ
Ω	Omega	ω
Ϡ	Sampi	ϡ

2.
φ – fife off of phone tuft toughed
χ – chorus kin chandelier candle
ψ – psalm upside corpse corps
ω – stove love board dough owe

3.
0. — 0 grapes (γρηψ)
5. — healed (῾ῑλδ)
8. — bored (βωρδ)
13. — grief (γρῑφ)
6. — look (λῠχ)
18. — friend (φρενδ)
16. — loads (λωζ)
15. — fuel (φῡλ)
2. — haste (ἡστ)
4. — thrift (θρῐφτ)
14. — thief (θῑφ)
17. — flops (φλαψ)
7. — known (νων)
9. — popes (ποψ)
1. — cleft (κλεφτ)
11. — heart (ἁρτ)
10. — roads (ρωζ)
3. — growth (γρωθ)
12. — gropes (γροψ)

A Complete Review of the Greek Alphabet, pages 98-101

1.

1. Digamma	Ϝ	Ϝ
2. Qoppa	Ϙ	ϙ
3. Sampi	Ϡ	ϡ

2.

1. Iota	Ι	ι	ͺ
2. Sigma	Σ	σ	ς

3.

1. Iota	Ι	ι, ͺ

1a. chin
1b. machine
1c. savior
1d. wait

2. Upsilon	Υ	υ

2a. put
2b. vacuum
2c. suave

4.

1. Alpha	Α	α

1a. yacht
1b. yawn

2. Gamma	Γ	γ

2a. gag
2b. sinking

3. Sigma	Σ	σ, ς

3a. hiss
3b. his

5.

1. (short) Epsilon	Ε	ε
(long) Eta	Η	η

1a. whet
1b. whey

2. (short) Omicron	Ο	ο
(long) Omega	Ω	ω

2a. oh
2b. owe

6.

1. Rough-Breather	ʽ

1a. hair

2. Smooth-Breather	ʼ

2a. heir

7.

0. — Beta (β)
11. — Tau (τ)
8. — Ksi (ξ)
9. — Pi (π)
14. — Psi (ψ)
12. — Phi (φ)
2. — Dzeta (ζ)
10. — Rho (ρ)
13. — Khi (χ)
1. — Delta (δ)
6. — Mu (μ)
3. — Theta (θ)
7. — Nu (ν)
4. — Kappa (κ)
5. — Lambda (λ)

0. — bob (β)
10. — rhetoric (ρ)
7. — noon (ν)
11. — totter (τ)
1. — dad (δ)
8. — axe (ξ)
3. — thin (θ)
9. — popper (π)
2. — adze (ζ)
5. — lull (λ)
4. — kicker (κ)
13. — loch (χ)
14. — lips (ψ)
6. — mom (μ)
12. — phosphor (φ)

GREEK VOWEL COMBINATIONS

Proper Diphthongs, pages 104-107

1.

αι – aisle isle I'll aye eye
sign sigh height buy
lie lye fly

ει – eight ate reign rein rain
veil vale

οι – oil loyal boy buoy

αυ – sauerkraut out doubt crowd

ευ – feud fewed cue view

ου – group fruit to too two through
due dew deuce do dude loop

2.

0. — eye (αἰ)
6. — feuds (φευζ)
7. — deuce (δους)
9. — how (ἁυ)
15. — baste (βειστ)
11. — bait (βειτ)
12. — royal (ροιλ)
16. — hewed (εὑδ)
13. — food (φουδ)
1. — foiled (φοιλδ)
3. — pride (πραιδ)
14. — bite (βαιτ)
4. — fruit (φρουτ)
5. — doubt (δαυτ)
2. — night (ναιτ)
8. — dowse (δαυς)
10. — frayed (φρειδ)

Improper Diphthongs, pages 108-111

1.

5. — coincide (κῳνσαιδ)
4. — pay inside (πῃνσαιδ)
1. — claw it (κλᾳτ)
6. — hoe it (ᾡτ)
2. — paw inside (πᾳνσαιδ)
3. — clay it (κλῃτ)

2.

7. — wheat (υἱτ)
5. — sweetly (συιτλῑ)
6. — no use (νωῡς)
2. — I owe you (αἰωῡ)
1. — straw unique (στρᾱῡνῑκ)
8. — law union (λᾱῡνιον)
4. — play euchre (πληῡκερ)
3. — hey you (ηὑ [ῡ])

Review of All Vowel Combinations, pages 114-115

1.

~~αε~~ ~~ωα~~ ~~ιο~~ ~~εα~~ ευ ~~αο~~ ~~ωω~~ ~~υη~~ ~~ιε~~ ~~αα~~ ῃ ~~ιυ~~
~~οω~~ ~~ιη~~ ~~υα~~ ~~εω~~ ωυ ~~υυ~~ ~~ωο~~ ~~ηω~~ ~~αη~~ ~~υο~~ ει
~~αω~~ ~~ιω~~ ~~ηη~~ οι αυ ~~υω~~ ~~ωε~~ ου ~~εη~~ ῳ ~~οα~~
~~οο~~ ~~εο~~ αι ᾳ ~~ηα~~ ~~εε~~ ~~ηε~~ ~~ιι~~ ~~ωη~~ ~~ηο~~ ηυ ~~ια~~ ~~οε~~
υι ~~οη~~ ~~υε~~

2.

αε ωα ιο εα εϋ αο ωω υη ιε αα ηϊ ιυ
οω ιη υα εω ωϋ υυ ωο ηω αη υο εϊ
αω ιω ηη οϊ αϋ υω ωε οϋ εη ωϊ οα
οο εο αϊ ᾳ ηα εε ηε ιι ωη ηο ηϋ ια οε
υϊ οη υε

3.

9. — gnaw you (νᾱυ)
13. — know you (νωυ)
7. — grew (γρου)
14. — wheel (υἱλ)
8. — saw it (σᾳτ)
11. — weigh unit (ὑηυνιτ)
12. — owe it (ᾡτ)
2. — kraut (κραυτ)
10. — say it (σῃτ)
3. — crate (κρειτ)
4. — feudal (φευδλ)
5. — ruined (ρυϊνδ)
1. — sight (σαιτ)
6. — Hoyle (οἱλ)